Simply Mama Cooks

FOR MY SONS DAX AND BO.
YOU ARE THE MOST AMAZING HUMANS I KNOW.
I LOVE YOU BOTH BEYOND MEASURE,
INFINITELY AND EVEN MORE THAN THAT.

FIRST EDITION

Design by Liliana Guia
Edited by Jessica Gilcrease

ISBN: 978-1-735-42070-7

Simply Mama Cooks

FOOD COOKED WITH A MAMA'S LOVE

Angelica Faz Jung

INTRODUCTION

My first memories of cooking and food are deeply rooted with my grandmothers. My paternal grandmother, Abuelita Faz, would always have large pots of simmering stewed meats on the stove. Rice, beans, tortillas and her favorite salsa were always ready for anyone that was hungry. In her kitchen, she had a small table pushed against the wall and her chair faced the front door. Her trusty coffee pot was always brewing fresh coffee for family and friends that would stop by for a plate or a visit. When it was time to make tamales, she would fill that same table with pounds of fresh masa and have the family gather around to help prepare the tamales. My best memories of her were holiday meals at her house.

I also remember playing with flour tortilla dough alongside my maternal grandmother, Abuelita Angelica. Her willingness to let me sit and play in her kitchen space meant the world to me. Most importantly, this gave me a love of cooking for my family at a very young age. It would be years later that I would finally try my hand at making my own flour tortillas using her method. The only issue would be trying to figure out the recipe. My Abuelita never measured anything. With many failed attempts and plenty of practice, I came up with just the right ratio of ingredients to replicate soft flour tortillas. I not only recreated tortillas just like hers, but I recreated a happy childhood memory. With that, I decided to continue to recreate and come up with recipes inspired from delicious home-cooked meals or happy moments in life.

Now that I am married with two growing sons, I find that making memories around the dinner table is a wonderful way to bond as a family. I love when a home-cooked meal becomes a household favorite or special request from my family. Sharing recipes became a hobby that turned into a career, and for that I am thankful. With the encouragement of my husband and patience of my children, I am able to cook, film and share my recipe videos on my YouTube channel and other social media platforms. I am not a professional cook, but I truly enjoy cooking. I love the process of learning and sharing recipes.

With the support of my growing social media following, I have decided to create and compile some of my recipes in a cookbook. This cookbook consists mainly of recipes I had growing up in a Mexican American family in Houston, Texas. I have also included some recipes I have learned as an adult that are family favorites.

If I had a motto for cooking, it would be something like the following, "Take what you know, embrace what you don't know and make it delicious!" There may be a recipe you want to recreate, but you may lack an ingredient. I say, use what you have and make it work. Do not let it stop you from making it your own and creating a delicious home-cooked meal. Do not let the lack of authenticity stop you from feeding your family and friends a meal from the heart. This is something my mother taught me long ago. Some of the best food I have ever eaten came from modest ingredients and novice cooking techniques made with loving intentions.

COOKING NOTES FROM ANGELICA

My approach to cooking is to make recipes simple so that when they are recreated, the recipe can be adjusted to your taste and preference. One thing I learned while growing up was that half of my family would complain of under seasoned food and the other half wanted less salt or spice. It made me understand that everyone has different tastes and preferences when it comes to seasoning food. I encourage you to season and make these recipes suitable for you.

I like to use bouillon powders in many of my recipes, but I understand that some prefer natural stocks and broth. You can substitute the water and bouillon powder for homemade or store bought broth. Then add salt to taste.

One dry seasoning I commonly use is chili powder. The type of chili powder is not spicy and is a blend with other dry seasonings. The types of chiles used are mild in spice.

I encourage you to enjoy the process of cooking and do not be afraid to improvise. Be sure to make these dishes and add your own spin to them. I hope you can recreate a dish that reminds you of a happy memory, a childhood meal or just — home. Maybe some of my favorite recipes can become yours.

TORTILLAS

SOFT FLOUR TORTILLAS

3 cups (400 g) all-purpose flour
1 tsp (5 g) salt
2 tsp (7.5 g) baking powder
1/3 cup (65 g) lard, shortening or butter
8 fl oz (236.5 ml) hot water

1. In a large bowl, combine flour, salt and baking powder.

2. Combine lard until the flour mixture is crumbly.

3. Add hot water and combine well until the dough ball forms.

4. Place the dough ball onto a lightly floured work surface.

5. Knead dough for 10 minutes or until the dough has a smooth surface and springs back to touch.

6. Divide dough into 12 to 14 dough balls, place back into bowl and cover with a damp cloth. Rest for at least 15 minutes.

7. Lightly dust the work surface and rolling pin with flour.

8. Roll out the dough ball into a thin circular shape. Then hang over the side of the bowl to rest while you continue to roll out 2 to 3 more tortillas before starting the cooking process.

9. Preheat a griddle or skillet on a medium high heat until it starts to develop wisps of smoke. Then place a tortilla on the griddle and cook for 15 seconds. If air pockets do not form, your heat source may need to be adjusted higher.

10. Flip and cook for another 15 seconds. Flip once more until the tortilla is cooked through. Then place into a tortilla warmer.

NOTES: If the dough seems too sticky to knead, add extra flour a tablespoon at a time until it is workable. If the dough seems too dry, then add more hot water a tablespoon at a time until dough comes together. If the dough shrinks back when rolling out, then the dough may need to rest longer. The overuse of flour when rolling out may result in a hard, dry tortilla. Kneading and resting the dough helps achieve air pockets when cooking. This recipe makes at least 12 tortillas. These are best eaten on the same day.

SOFT CORN TORTILLAS

1 1/2 cups (175 g) instant corn flour for masa
1/2 tsp (2.5 g) salt
2 Tbsp (15 g) cornstarch
8 fl oz (236.5 ml) hot water

1. In a large bowl, combine instant corn flour, salt and cornstarch.
2. Add hot water and mix vigorously for 10 minutes.
3. Divide into 12 dough balls and cover with a damp cloth to prevent the dough from drying out. Rest for 15 minutes.
4. Cut two pieces of wax or parchment paper 9 inches in diameter.
5. Place one piece of wax paper on the bottom plate of a tortilla press.
6. Then add a masa dough ball in the center of the press, cover with a second piece of wax paper, and press out into a tortilla. You can also use two flat-bottomed pans or plates to press out.
7. Gently lay your pressed dough onto a hot griddle and cook for 10 seconds on the first side.
8. Flip and cook for 10 to 15 seconds on the second side.
9. Flip once more and press the center of the tortilla to help puff up. Once it puffs or cooks for another 5 seconds, remove from the griddle. Place the cooked tortilla into a tortilla warmer.

NOTES: If the dough seems too dry, then add more hot water a tablespoon at a time. Resting is key to allow the hot water to completely saturate the instant corn flour. Cooked tortillas should be covered to maintain moisture and warmth.

SOFT RED CORN TORTILLAS

3 dried guajillo chiles (18 g)
1/2 cup (120 ml) water (for chile purée)
2 1/2 cups (300 g) instant corn flour (for masa)
1 tsp (5 g) salt
3 Tbsp (22.5 g) corn starch
2 cups (473 ml) hot water

1. First remove the stems and seeds from guajillo chiles. Rinse and wash them well to remove any debris.

2. Add cleaned chiles to a small pot of water, bring to a boil, turn off heat, cover with a lid, and steep for 30 minutes or until softened.

3. Remove the chiles from the pot and discard the soaking liquid. Add softened chiles and 1/2 cup water to a blender and puree. Strain the puree and set aside until needed.

4. In a large bowl combine instant corn flour, salt and cornstarch. Then add hot water and chile puree. Mix vigorously for 10 minutes.

5. Divide into 18 to 20 dough balls and cover with damp cloth to prevent dough from drying out. Rest for 15 minutes.

6. Cut two pieces of wax or parchment paper 9 inches in diameter.

7. Place one piece of wax paper on the bottom plate of a tortilla press

8. Then add a masa dough ball in the center of the tortilla press, cover with a second piece of wax paper and press out into a tortilla. You can also use two flat-bottomed pans or plates to press out.

9. Gently lay your pressed dough onto a hot griddle and cook for 10 seconds on the first side.

10. Flip and cook for 10 to 15 seconds on the second side.

11. Flip once more and press the center of the tortilla to help puff up. Once it puffs or cooks for another 5 seconds, remove from the griddle. Place the cooked tortilla into a tortilla warmer.

NOTES: If the dough seems too dry, then add more hot water a tablespoon at a time. Resting is key to allow the hot water to completely saturate the instant corn flour. Cooked tortillas should be covered to maintain moisture and warmth.

SALSAS
& DIPS

ROASTED GUACAMOLE DIP

1 jalapeño (45 g)
1/2 small onion (80 g)
3 cloves garlic (12 g)
1 Roma tomato (60 g)
1 scallion (15 g)
4 small avocados
3 Tbsp (45 ml) fresh lime juice
1/3 cup (30 g) fresh chopped cilantro
salt and pepper to taste

1. Place jalapeño, onion and garlic with skin on a small baking sheet and broil for a minute or until slightly charred. For less spice, remove the seeds and veins from jalapeño.

2. Remove the charred jalapeño, onion and garlic from the broiler. Cool and chop.

3. Cut the Roma tomato in half, scoop out the seeds and dice. Chop the scallion using the green and white part.

4. Add chopped jalapeño, onion, minced garlic, diced tomato, chopped scallion to a bowl and combine.

5. Cut each avocado in half around the pit. Remove the pit and scoop out the flesh with a spoon. Dice and place into a bowl. Save one pit for later use.

6. Now add fresh lime juice, salt and pepper to taste. Then combine well.

7. After mixing, taste for salt and adjust if needed. Place the pit in the center of the dip and serve.

NOTES: For an extra spicy dip, substitute the jalapeño for a serrano pepper and leave in the seeds. For a creamy dip, mash or puree the avocado with the lime juice first. Then combine the rest of the ingredients.

MAMA'S FAVORITE SALSA

5 dried guajillo chiles (30 g)
2 dried chile arbol (3 g)
2 tomatillos (85 g)
1/2 small onion (70 g)
2 cloves garlic (8 g)
1/2 tsp (2 g) chicken bouillon powder
1/2 cup (120 ml) water
salt to taste

1. Remove the stems and seeds from guajillo chiles. Only remove the stems from the chile arbol and leave the rest whole with seeds and all. Rinse to remove any debris.

2. Add the cleaned chiles to a small pot of water and bring to a boil. Then turn off the heat, cover with a lid and steep for 30 minutes or until softened.

3. Remove the husks from the tomatillos and rinse.

4. On a preheated griddle, add 2 Tbsp cooking oil, onion, tomatillos and garlic with the skin on. Char for 3 to 5 minutes using a medium high heat. Remove and set aside until needed.

5. Remove chiles from the pot and discard soaking liquid. Add the softened chiles to a blender.

6. Peel the skin from garlic and add it to blender along with onion, tomatillos, chicken bouillon powder and water. Then puree.

7. Pour the salsa into a bowl, taste for salt, adjust to your preference, mix and serve.

EASY ROASTED GREEN SALSA

1 lb (454 g) tomatillos
2 jalapeños (90 g)
1 medium onion (120 g)
4 cloves (16 g) garlic
salt to taste

1. First remove the husks from the tomatillos and rinse to remove any debris. Then cut in half.

2. Cut the stems from the jalapeños and cut the onion in half. Be sure to leave the skin on all garlic.

3. Place the tomatillos, onion, jalapeños and garlic on a baking sheet. Then broil until charred. The broil time will vary.

4. Remove ingredients from the broiler once charred, place them into a blender and puree.

5. Pour salsa into a bowl. Add salt to your taste and serve.

EASY EVERYDAY SALSA

1/2 lb (227 g) Roma tomatoes
2 jalapeños (90 g)
1 medium onion (120 g)
4 cloves (16 g) garlic
salt to taste

1. To prepare ingredients, rinse the tomatoes well, remove stems from jalapeños and remove skins from garlic.

2. Place all of the tomatoes, onion, garlic and jalapeños in a pot of water. Then bring it to a boil.

3. Boil for 8 to 10 minutes.

4. Remove the ingredients from the boiling liquid, place into a blender and blend until it's to your desired consistency.

5. Pour into a bowl, add salt to taste and serve.

MAMA'S FAKE-OUT GUACAMOLE SALSA

2 tomatillos (85 g)
1 jalapeño (45 g)
1/2 medium onion (90 g)
1 medium Mexican squash (220 g)
3 cloves garlic (12 g)
1 Tbsp (15 ml) cooking oil
salt to taste

1. Remove the husks from the tomatillos and rinse to remove any debris. Then cut in half.
2. Cut the stems from the jalapeños. Then cut the onion and Mexican squash into large chunks, and be sure to leave the skin on all garlic.
3. Place tomatillos, jalapeños, garlic, onion and Mexican squash on a baking sheet.
4. Roast ingredients in a preheated oven at 450 °F / 232 °C for 15 minutes.
5. Remove skin from the garlic. Then place all of the roasted ingredients, oil and salt to taste into the blender.
6. Puree until smooth and emulsified. Then taste for salt and adjust to your preference.

NOTES: The combination of the roasted ingredients and oil creates a creamy texture much like pureed avocado salsa, but without the oxidation. For a spicy salsa, add serrano peppers in place of the jalapeño.

ENTREES

STOVETOP CARNE GUISADA

1 1/2 lbs (680 g) beef chuck roast meat
3 fresh Roma tomatoes (180 g)
1 small onion (100 g)
3 cloves fresh garlic (15 g)
3 Tbsp (45 ml) cooking oil
1/2 tsp (2.5 g) salt

1/2 tsp (1 g) black pepper
1 tsp (3 g) ground cumin
1 Tbsp (10 g) beef bouillon powder
3 Tbsp (30 g) all-purpose flour
3 cups (709 ml) water

1. Prepare the ingredients by cutting beef into 1/2 inch pieces, small dice the tomatoes, finely chop the onions and finely mince the garlic.

2. In a preheated skillet with a lid, add cooking oil and brown the meat over a high heat. Remove the browned meat from the skillet and set aside until needed.

3. Lower the heat to medium and in the same skillet sauté the chopped onions, tomatoes and garlic until the tomatoes have softened and the onions are translucent.

4. Now add browned meat back into the skillet with the sauté and combine well over a medium heat. Add salt, pepper, ground cumin and beef bouillon powder. Then combine.

5. Now sprinkle flour evenly over everything in the skillet, cook and combine well for 1 to 2 minutes or until a golden brown crust forms at the bottom of the pan.

6. Add in water slowly while mixing. A sauce should form.

7. Bring to a gentle simmer, cover with a lid, lower the heat and simmer for at least 1 hour or until the meat is tender. Stir occasionally while it simmers to prevent the bottom from burning. Adjust heat source accordingly. Extra water may be needed during the cooking process if meat needs to cook longer to become tender.

8. Once the meat is tender and the gravy has thickened, turn off the heat. Set for ten minutes and serve.

NOTES: You can substitute the beef bouillon powder and water with beef broth. Be sure to adjust the salt and seasonings to your taste and preference. When the cook time is done, the sauce should thicken like a gravy. If the sauce is too thin, uncover and continue simmering until the sauce has thickened. This makes 4 servings.

STOVETOP CARNE ASADA

1/2 cup (120 ml) low sodium soy sauce
1/4 cup (60 ml) fresh juice of orange
1/4 cup (60 ml) fresh juice of lime
1 tsp (3 g) onion powder
1 tsp (3 g) garlic powder
1 tsp (2.3 g) smoked paprika
1 1/2 tsp (5 g) sugar
1/2 tsp (1 g) black pepper
1 small onion (90 g)
4 cloves of fresh garlic (16 g)
2 1/2 lbs (1.13 kg) beef skirt meat or flank steak

1. In a bowl, combine soy sauce, orange juice, lime juice, all dried spices and sugar. Then mix well to make a marinade.

2. Slice the onion into rings and slice the garlic.

3. In a bowl or a large plastic storage bag, combine the meat, onions, garlic and marinade.

4. Combine and coat the meat well. If using a glass dish, layer the meat, onions, garlic and marinade.

5. Place in the refrigerator and marinate for 2 to 3 hours. If using a tough cut of beef, marinate overnight for best results.

6. Remove the marinated meat and set on the counter 15 to 20 minutes before cooking to remove the chill.

7. Preheat your griddle, pan or skillet on a medium high heat until the pan is hot.

8. Sear the meat on each side for 2 to 3 minutes. Cook time will vary depending on the desired doneness you prefer.

9. Once the meat is cooked to your preferred doneness, remove from the skillet onto a plate or baking sheet and cover. Then rest for 10 minutes before slicing and serving.

NOTES: When slicing, be sure to cut against the grain. This makes 4 to 6 servings.

EASY BEEF CHILI

1 medium onion (120 g)
5 cloves fresh garlic (20 g)
1 chipotle pepper in Adobo sauce (13 g)
3 Tbsp (45 ml) cooking oil
3 lbs (1.36 kg) ground beef (85/15 meat to fat ratio)
6 Tbsp (40 g) chili powder
3 tsp (7 g) smoked paprika
3 tsp (9 g) garlic powder
3 tsp (9 g) onion powder
3 tsp (7 g) ground cumin
3 Tbsp (49.5 g) tomato paste
7 cups (1.65 L) beef broth
2 Tbsp (20 g) Adobo sauce from can of chipotle peppers
1/4 cup (40 g) cornstarch
3 Tbsp (45 ml) cold water
two 15 oz cans cooked pinto beans (optional)
salt and pepper to taste

1. Prepare the ingredients by finely chopping the onion, finely mincing the garlic and finely chopping the chipotle pepper.

2. In a preheated heavy bottomed 6 quart pot with a lid, add the cooking oil and brown the meat over a medium high heat for 5 to 7 minutes.

3. Lower the heat to medium and add the chopped onions and garlic until the onions have soften and become translucent.

4. Now add all the dry seasonings and spices to the meat and combine well.

5. Add in the tomato paste, combine and cook for 1 or 2 minutes.

6. Next add the beef broth, chopped chipotle pepper and adobo sauce. Then mix well.

7. Bring to a gentle boil, cover with a lid, lower the heat and simmer for 1 hour. Stir occasionally throughout the simmer to prevent the bottom from burning. Adjust heat source accordingly.

8. In a small bowl, combine the cornstarch and cold water to create a slurry.

9. Add slurry into the chili and stir.

10. If adding beans, then be sure to drain and rinse canned beans. Combine and mix into the chili. Continue cooking for an additional 15 minutes uncovered and serve.

NOTES: This chili tastes even better the next day. This makes 8 to 10 servings.

TEX-MEX GROUND BEEF ENCHILADAS

2 Tbsp (30 ml) cooking oil
1 lb (454 g) lean ground beef
1/4 cup (40 g) onion diced
2 garlic cloves (10 g) minced
3/4 tsp (3.75 g) salt
1/4 tsp black pepper
1/2 tsp (1 g) ground cumin
14 corn tortillas
12 oz (340.5 g) shredded cheddar or Colby jack cheese
1/4 cup (59 ml) cooking oil

RED SAUCE
1/4 (59 ml) cooking oil
1/4 cup (35 g) all purpose flour
2 Tbsp (12 g) chili powder
1 Tbsp (10 g) granulated chicken or beef bouillon powder
1 tsp (4 g) garlic powder
1 tsp (4 g) onion powder
1/4 tsp (.75 g) ground cumin
2 cups (473 ml) water (room temperature)

1. In a preheated skillet over a medium heat, add cooking oil, ground beef, diced onions, minced garlic, salt, pepper and ground cumin. Then brown until the meat is cooked through. Set aside until ready to assemble enchiladas.

2. In a medium to small pan or griddle, add 1/3 cup of cooking oil and preheat on a medium low heat.

3. Now pass each corn tortilla through the hot oil for only 3 seconds on each side and remove from the pan. Repeat the process until all the tortillas are heated through. Set aside until ready to assemble the enchiladas.

4. To make the sauce, in a medium sized pan, add cooking oil then evenly sprinkle flour to make a roux. Cook over a medium heat for 45 seconds to 1 minute.

5. While continuing to stir, add chili powder, bouillon powder, garlic powder, onion powder and ground cumin.

6. Now slowly add in water while constantly whisking.

7. Continue to stir and mix until sauce thickens. Then remove from heat.

8. In a 9 inch by 13 inch baking dish, add 1/3 cup of enchilada sauce and spread all over the bottom of the baking dish.

9. Reserve a cup of cheese in a small bowl for later use.

10. To assemble, fill a corn tortilla with cooked ground beef and shredded cheese, and tightly roll. Place rolled enchilada seam side down in the sauced baking dish and continue the process until all enchiladas are rolled out.

11. Now pour the sauce over the enchiladas and spread evenly to cover any exposed corn tortilla.

12. Take the reserved shredded cheese and evenly sprinkle on the top of the enchiladas.

13. Cover the baking dish with aluminum foil and bake in a preheated oven at 375 °F / 190 °C for 20 minutes. Then remove the foil and bake for an additional 10 to 15 minutes.

14. Remove from the oven and allow to set for at least 20 minutes, then serve.

NOTES: You can substitute the beef bouillon powder and water with 2 cups of beef broth and salt to taste. This makes 4 to 6 servings.

MAMA'S ARROZ CON POLLO

1 cup (160 g) long grain rice (rinsed and dried)
1 1/2 to 2 lbs (680 g to 907 g) bone in chicken thigh
2 Tbsp cooking oil
2 cloves garlic minced (13 g)
2 cups (473 ml) water
1 Tbsp (10 g) chicken bouillon powder
2/3 cup (157 ml) crushed tomato
1/2 tsp (2 g) onion powder
1/2 tsp (2 g) garlic powder
1/2 tsp (1.5 g) ground cumin
1/2 tsp (1 g) black pepper
1 medium sized onion (175 g)

RUB
1 tsp (5 g) salt
1 tsp (2.3 g) paprika
1/2 tsp (1.5 g) onion powder
1/2 tsp (1.5 g) garlic powder
1/2 tsp (1.5 g) salt-free lemon pepper

1. Rinse and drain the rice. Set aside in a fine mesh strainer until ready to use.

2. Season chicken on both sides with rub or seasonings of your choice.

3. In a large preheated skillet, add 2 Tbsp cooking oil, place chicken skin side down and brown for 3 minutes on each side using a medium heat.

4. Once chicken is browned on each side, cover with a lid, lower the heat to a low setting and continue cooking chicken for 10 to 12 minutes.

5. Once the cook time is up, remove the chicken from the skillet and set aside until later use.

6. Turn the heat to a medium setting and in the same pan add the rice and toast for 5 minutes or until golden brown. Cook time will vary.

7. Next add minced fresh garlic to the rice and sauté for 1 minute.

8. Combine water and chicken bouillon powder. Then pour into the skillet with toasted rice, stir and try to remove any brown bits from the bottom while stirring.

9. Next add crushed tomatoes, onion powder, garlic powder, ground cumin and black pepper, and combine.

10. Now arrange the chicken skin side up into the skillet.

11. Cut the onion in to large wedge chunks and place in between the pieces of chicken.

12. Bring to a gentle boil, cover with a lid, set the heat to a low setting and simmer for 20 to 22 minutes.

13. After the cook time, turn off the heat. DO NOT lift the lid and allow it to set covered for 5 to 10 minutes.

14. Then uncover and serve.

NOTES: You can substitute the chicken bouillon powder and water with chicken broth or stock and salt to your preference. It is important to allow the rice to set after the cook time. The rice will continue to cook with the residual heat and absorb any liquid left in the pan. This makes 4 servings.

CHEESY LAYERED CHICKEN ENCHILADAS

2 lbs (908 g) cooked chicken chopped
18 corn tortillas
1/3 cup (77 ml) cooking oil (for heating tortillas)
14 oz (396 g) shredded mozzarella or Monterey jack cheese

RED SAUCE
5 Tbsp (75 ml) cooking oil
6 Tbsp (60 g) all purpose flour
1 Tbsp (16 g) tomato paste
2 Tbsp (12 g) chili powder
1 tsp (4 g) garlic powder
1 tsp (4 g) onion powder
1/2 tsp (1.5 g) ground cumin
3 1/2 cups (828 ml) low sodium chicken broth
1 tsp (5 g) salt (or to taste)

1. To make the sauce, in a medium to large sized pan, add cooking oil then evenly sprinkle flour to make a roux. Cook over a medium heat for 45 seconds to 1 minute.

2. While continuing to stir, add tomato paste and combine. Next add chili powder, garlic powder, onion powder and ground cumin, and combine.

3. Now slowly add in chicken broth while constantly whisking. Continue to stir and mix until sauce thickens. Then remove from heat.

4. Next add chili powder, garlic powder, onion powder, ground cumin and salt to taste, then combine. Simmer until thickened.

5. Reserve a cup and a half of cheese in a small bowl for later use.

6. In a 9 inch by 13 inch baking dish, add 1/2 cup of enchilada sauce and spread all over the bottom of the baking dish.

7. Layer 6 corn tortillas at the bottom of the baking dish and evenly add a layer of chicken, cheese and 3/4 cup of sauce. Repeat the process 2 more times. On the last layer, add the remainder of the sauce and then sprinkle the reserved cheese.

8. Cover the baking dish with foil and bake in a preheated oven at 375 °F / 190 °C for 20 minutes. Then remove foil and bake for an additional 10 to 15 minutes.

9. Remove from the oven and allow to set for at least 20 minutes, then serve.

NOTES: You can substitute the chicken broth and salt with 3 1/2 cups of water and 1 1/2 Tbsp of chicken bouillon powder. Allowing your layered enchiladas to set prevents the layers from sliding apart when serving. This makes at least 9 servings.

SIMPLE STOVE TOP RED ENCHILADAS

10 oz (283 g) queso fresco
10 oz (283 g) Oaxaca cheese
2/3 cup (80 g) diced onions
1/3 cup (40 g) chopped scallions
1/3 cup (20 g) chopped cilantro (optional)
1/2 tsp (1 g) black pepper
1/3 cup (77 ml) cooking oil (to heat tortillas)
14 to 16 corn tortillas

RED SAUCE

10 dried guajillo chiles (60 g)
1/2 small onion (80 g)
3 cloves fresh garlic (12 g)
1/2 small onion (80 g)
3 cups (709 ml) low sodium chicken broth
1 tsp (4 g) garlic powder
1 tsp (4 g) onion powder
1/2 tsp (1.5 g) ground cumin
salt to taste

1. To prepare the filling, in a large bowl, shred the Oaxaca cheese, crumble the queso fresco, and add diced onion, chopped scallions, and black pepper. Then combine well. Set aside in the refrigerator until ready to use.

2. In a medium to small pan or griddle, add 1/3 cup of cooking oil and preheat on a medium low heat.

3. Now pass each corn tortilla through the hot oil for only 3 seconds on each side, remove from pan and repeat the process until all of the tortillas are heated through. Set aside until ready to assemble enchiladas.

4. To make sauce, first remove the stems and seeds from the guajillo chiles. Rinse and wash well to remove any debris.

5. Add the cleaned chiles to a medium to small pot of water, bring to a boil, turn off heat, cover with a lid and steep for 30 minutes or until softened.

6. Remove the chiles from the pot and discard the soaking liquid. Add softened chiles, half of a chopped small onion, chopped garlic, and 2 cups of chicken broth to a blender.

7. Blend until pureed well.

8. In a preheated medium pan or pot, add 2 Tbsp cooking oil and pour the puree through a fine wire mesh strainer directly into the pan.

9. Add the remaining chicken broth, garlic powder, onion powder and ground cumin. Then combine and gently simmer for 5 to 7 minutes. Taste for seasoning and salt, then adjust to your taste and preference.

10. To assemble, take a corn tortilla, carefully dip into enchilada sauce, then fill with cheese mixture, roll and place seam side down on to a plate. Roll four enchiladas, then garnish with more cheese and fresh toppings of your choice.

11. Another option is to dip the tortilla and place on a preheated oiled griddle, add cheese mixture, carefully fold over with a spatula and lightly fry until cheese is melted. Then plate and garnish.

NOTES: You can use shredded chicken or beef for your filling. After plating the enchiladas, you can pour over extra sauce then top with garnishes. You can assemble your enchiladas without hand dipping. To do this, place in a baking dish, pour over sauce and extra cheese, and bake until cheese is melted for an easier method. This serves 4 to 6 servings.

TENDER MEAT FILLED TAMALES

CHILE PUREE

8 dried guajillo chiles (55 g)
2 dried pasilla chiles (20 g)
2 dried ancho chiles (18 g)
1/2 small onion (80 g)
3 cloves garlic (12 g)
1 cup (236.5 ml) broth or water

MASA

4 cups (475 g) instant corn flour for masa
2 tsp (10 g) salt
2 1/2 tsp (10 g) baking powder
1 cup (200 g) lard or shortening
1/3 cup (80 ml) chile puree
3 cups (709 ml) hot broth or hot water

MEAT FILLING

2 1/2 lbs (1.13 kg) cooked beef, chicken or pork
2 cups (500 ml) chile puree
1 tsp salt (5 g) or salt to taste

PREPARE THE CORN HUSKS

1. Separate and rinse 50 corn husks.

2. Add to a large 12 quart pot with water and bring to a boil.

3. Boil husks for 15 minutes.

4. Turn off the heat, cover with a lid and soak for at least one hour or until ready to use.

5. Once ready to use, remove from water and place in a large strainer upright to allow excess water to run off.

MAKE THE CHILE PUREE

1. Remove the stems and seeds from all of the dried chiles.

2. Rinse for any debris.

3. Place cleaned chiles, onion and garlic in a pot and cover with water.

4. Bring the pot to a boil, turn off heat, cover with a lid and soak chiles for at least 30 minutes or until softened.

5. Remove the softened chiles, onion and garlic from the pot and place in a blender. Discard soaking liquid.

6. Add 1 cup of broth or water to the blender and puree well.

7. Pour chile puree through fine wire mesh strainer.

8. Reserve 1/3 cup of chile puree for masa. The rest is to be used for meat filling.

MAKE THE MEAT FILLING

1. Chop or shred meat to desired texture.

2. To a preheated pan, add 2 Tbsp oil and strained chile puree. Salt to taste and simmer for 5 minutes on a medium low heat.

3. Now add chopped meat, combine well and continue to cook for 3 to 5 minutes. Then taste for seasoning and salt.

4. Turn off the heat and set aside until ready to assemble tamales.

MAKE THE MASA

1. In a large bowl, combine instant corn flour, salt and baking powder.

2. Add lard and combine well.

3. Now add hot broth or water and 1/3 cup chile puree. Then whip with hand or mixer until well combined and fluffy.

4. Cover with a damp cloth to prevent masa dough from drying out until ready to use.

CONTINUE TO PAGE 34

ASSEMBLE AND COOK THE TAMALES

1. Take one presoaked corn husk and spread 3 to 4 Tbsp of masa on the smooth side of the corn husk, leaving 1/2 an inch of shape from the top.

2. Next add the meat filling and enclose the tamal overlapping one side of the corn husk over the other.

3. Now take the bottom of the corn husk and fold up towards the seam.

4. Continue the process until all of the tamales are assembled. This recipe will make at least 40 to 45 tamales depending on the ratio of masa to meat filling you use and prefer.

5. In a 16 to 20 quart steamer pot for tamales, add 2 liters of water to the bottom and place the steamer insert over the water. Be sure the water does not come over the steamer plate insert.

6. Now place a small heat proof bowl in the center to help arrange your tamales upright stacked against each other.

7. Cover your tamales with any extra corn husks and a damp tea cloth.

8. Cover with the lid, bring water to a rolling boil, then lower heat to a medium heat and cook for at least 1 hour and 15 minutes or until your tamal comes out easily from the corn husk. Cook time may vary.

9. Once the tamales are ready, turn off the heat and let the tamales set in the pot for 20 minutes. Then remove from the pot and serve.

NOTES: This makes at least 40 to 45 tamales. Be sure to check for my **Slow Cooker Beef** recipe, **Slow Cooker Pork** recipe and **Easy Baked Chicken** recipe which works well for the cooked meat in this recipe.

EASY OVEN BAKED CHICKEN

2 1/2 tsp (12.5 g) salt
2 tsp (5 g) paprika
2 tsp (8 g) onion powder
2 tsp (8 g) garlic powder
2 tsp (8 g) salt-free lemon pepper
3 lbs (1.36 kg) bone in chicken thighs or legs

1. In a small bowl, add salt, paprika, onion powder, garlic powder and lemon pepper. Then combine well.

2. Using all of the seasoning mixture, season the chicken all over and place on a large baking sheet lined with parchment paper.

3. Next place the chicken in a preheated oven at 375 °F / 190 °C and bake for 50 to 55 minutes or until the internal temperature reaches 165 °F / 74 °C.

4. Once the chicken is done, remove from the oven and allow to rest for 15 minutes. Then serve.

NOTES: This recipe makes 4 to 6 servings. Be sure that the chicken is completely thawed. If baking cold or partially frozen chicken, the cook time will vary.

CJ'S FAVORITE MOLÉ SAUCE

10 (50 g) guajillo chiles
2 (20 g) pasilla chiles
4 (45 g) ancho chiles
3 (274 g) Roma tomatoes
2 (135 g) tomatillos
7 (20 g) cloves of garlic
2 corn tortillas
1 small onion (130 g)
6 to 7 (55 g) prunes (you can sub with 1/3 cup raisins)
1 tsp (1g) Mexican oregano
1 chipotle chile in adobo (13 g)
7 cups (1.66 L) low sodium chicken broth
10 oz (283.5 g) 60% bittersweet chocolate
1/2 cup (120 g) sunflower butter (or peanut butter)
1/8 tsp ground cinnamon
pinch of ground clove
3 Tbsp (30 g) sugar
3 Tbsp (45 ml) cooking oil
salt to taste

1. Rinse chiles. Then remove their stems and seeds.

2. Broil cleaned chiles, onion, tomatoes, tomatillos and garlic with skin on. Also broil corn tortillas until charred and toasted. The chiles will char quickly, so remove first.

3. Place the toasted chiles in a bowl, cover with boiling hot water and steep for at least 30 minutes or until softened.

4. In a blender, add softened chiles, tomatoes, onions, garlic, tomatillos, corn tortillas, prunes, Mexican oregano, optional chipotle chili in adobo sauce and 2 cups chicken broth. Then puree well until smooth.

5. Strain puree by passing through a fine wire mesh strainer.

6. In a preheated 6 quart pot, add cooking oil and strained chile puree mixture.

7. Bring to a gentle simmer then add chocolate, sunflower butter, ground cinnamon, ground clove, sugar and 1 tsp of salt to start with. Also add 3 to 4 more cups of chicken broth as needed. This recipe uses 6 to 7 cups of chicken broth depending on your preference of sauce viscosity.

8. Once the molé sauce is mixed well and at a gentle simmer, taste for salt and adjust to preference. Then cover with a lid, lower the heat and continue to simmer for at least 30 minutes while stirring every 15 minutes. Then serve over baked chicken.

NOTES: This recipe makes at least 1.5 liters of sauce. You can serve this over **Easy Baked Chicken** and a side of **Easy Mexican Rice**.

CREAMY GARLIC MUSHROOM CHICKEN

1 1/2 tsp (7 g) salt
1 tsp (4 g) salt-free lemon pepper
1 tsp (4 g) garlic powder
1 tsp (4 g) onion powder
2 lbs (907 g) boneless skinless chicken breast
2 Tbsp (30 ml) cooking oil
8 oz (227 g) baby bella mushrooms sliced
4 tbsp (56.5 g) unsalted butter
half of small onion (60 g)
3 cloves garlic (12 g)
1 Tbsp (3 g) fresh rosemary
1 Tbsp (3 g) fresh thyme
1 Tbsp (3 g) fresh parsley
1 Tbsp (3 g) fresh chives
3 cups (709 ml) heavy cream
2 oz (56.5 g) grated parmesan cheese
1/4 tsp (1.25 g) salt
1/2 tsp (1 g) pepper

1. In a small bowl combine salt, salt-free lemon pepper, garlic powder and onion powder. Then mix well.

2. Season the chicken on both sides with the seasoning mix.

3. Preheat a large skillet over a medium heat, add cooking oil and 2 Tbsp unsalted butter.

4. Once the butter is melted, place the chicken in a skillet and brown and cook each side for 2 to 3 minutes.

5. Once the chicken is done, remove, cover tightly with foil and set aside until needed.

6. Now raise the heat to a medium high heat, add 1 Tbsp butter and sliced mushrooms. Then sauté until browned.

7. Lower the heat to a medium setting, add another 1 Tbsp of butter and finely diced onions. Sauté until onions are translucent.

8. Now add finely minced garlic, a pinch of salt and pepper to taste. Continue cooking for 1 minute.

9. Add fresh rosemary, thyme, parsley and chives. Sauté for another minute.

10. Lower the heat, add heavy cream, combine well and bring to a gentle simmer. Be sure to work with a low heat when adding the cream to avoid burning.

11. Next add grated parmesan cheese and combine well.

12. Add the chicken back into the pan and continue to gently simmer for another 5 minutes, turn off the heat, cover and let sit for 5 minutes, then serve.

NOTES: This makes 4 servings. Serve this with your favorite pasta, potatoes or steamed rice.

CRISPY CHILE RELLENOS

6 fresh poblano peppers
1 lb (454 g) russet potatoes
1 clove of garlic (5 g)
1 1/2 Tbsp (21 g) unsalted butter
1/2 tsp (1.25 g) smoked paprika
8 oz (227 g) mozzarella cheese shredded
salt and pepper to taste
12 toothpicks
1/2 cup (70 g) all-purpose flour (dredging for stuffed peppers)
6 chilled large eggs (separated whites from yolks)
Cooking oil for fry

PREPARE THE PEPPERS

1. Completely char the skin of the poblano peppers by placing them directly on your stove top burner flame and turning until outside skin is charred and blistered. Try to char skin quickly as this process can overcook the peppers making them mushy. Also be sure to work in a well ventilated area or working space when charring.

2. Place all of the charred peppers in a large bowl, cover with cling film and allow to set for 15 to 20 minutes.

3. After the charred peppers have set, start peeling and wiping off the charred skin.

4. After peeling off charred skin, make a small vertical slit. Be sure not to pierce the back side of the pepper. Remove the seeds, rinse and pat dry. Set peppers aside until ready to stuff.

PREPARE THE FILLING

1. Peel, rinse and chop potatoes into large chunks.

2. In a pot, add peeled chopped potatoes, one clove of peeled garlic and water covering the potatoes by half an inch. Bring water to a boil and cook until potatoes are fork tender.

3. Once the potatoes are tender, drain the water and return potatoes and garlic to the pot. Add unsalted butter, smoked paprika, salt and pepper, then mash well. Once the potatoes have cooled, add shredded cheese and mix.

ENTREES

FILL THE PEPPERS

1. Take each cleaned pepper and stuff with the potato cheese filling. Now take two toothpicks, close and secure seam.

2. On a large plate add all purpose flour. Now completely dredge and coat each stuffed pepper.

3. Place the stuffed and dredged pepper on a baking sheet and repeat the process until all of the peppers are done.

PREPARE THE EGG BATTER

1. Between two bowls, separate egg yolks from egg whites.

2. In a large chilled bowl, add the egg whites. With a hand mixer, beat until stiff peaks start to form.

3. Once stiff peaks form, add egg yolks one by one and continue mixing until combined well.

COOK THE STUFFED PEPPERS

1. Take each stuffed and dredged pepper and dip into the egg batter, coating it completely. Then quickly and carefully place in a preheated pan with 1/2 inch deep of fry oil. Fry oil should be at 350 °F / 176 °C.

2. Once the first side is cooked and golden brown, using 2 spatulas, carefully flip to the other side. Continue to fry each stuffed and battered pepper until the egg batter is cooked and golden brown.

3. When removing the cooked stuffed pepper from oil, carefully place it on a baking sheet with a cooling rack to allow any residual oil to run off. Repeat the process until all are fried.

NOTES: The flour dredge helps the fluffy egg batter adhere to the flesh of the pepper. Be sure the fry oil is preheated well. This will ensure a light crispy exterior to the chile rellenos. Be sure to remove the toothpicks before serving. This makes 3 to 4 servings.

EASY PICADILLO FOR TACOS

2 Tbsp cooking oil
½ small onion (80 g) chopped
2 medium potatoes (275 g) cubed
half of a medium carrot (50 g) diced
half of a small bell pepper (65 g) diced
3/4 tsp (3.5 g) salt
3 cloves garlic (13 g) minced
1 to 1 1/2 cups (115 g) fresh sweet corn kernels
1 medium squash or zucchini (175 g) chopped
1 lb (454 g) lean ground beef
1/2 tsp (2 g) garlic powder
1/2 tsp (2 g) onion powder
1/4 tsp (.5 g) paprika
1/4 tsp (.5 g) pepper to taste
1 1/4 cups (295. 5 ml) beef broth
1/3 cup (79 ml) tomato sauce

1. In a preheated large pan or skillet, add 2 Tbsp cooking oil and chopped onions. Using a medium heat, sauté until onions are translucent.

2. Now add cubed potatoes, diced carrot, diced bell pepper and a pinch of salt. Then continue to sauté for 3 to 5 minutes.

3. Next add minced garlic, fresh sweet corn kernels and diced zucchini. Continue to sauté for another 2 minutes.

4. Create an empty space in the center of your skillet, add the ground beef and start to break apart. Once the beef is broken up, add garlic powder, onion powder, paprika, black pepper and salt. Combine well and continue to cook for 5 to 7 minutes.

5. Add beef broth and tomato sauce, then combine well. Taste the broth and adjust any seasoning to your preference.

6. Bring to a gentle boil, cover with a lid, lower the heat and simmer for 20 minutes or until carrots and potatoes are cooked through.

7. For a less soupy picadillo, after 20 minutes of cooking time, remove the lid and continue cooking for an additional 10 minutes to reduce liquid in the pan. This method works great if using picadillo for tacos.

NOTES: This makes 4 to 6 servings or up to at least 8 to 10 tacos.

EASY MEXICAN STYLE CHORIZO

5 dried guajillo chiles (30 g)
3 cloves of garlic (12 g)
1 dried bay leaf
1/2 tsp (.5 g) dried Mexican oregano
1/4 cup (60 ml) apple cider vinegar
1 lb (454 g) ground pork or beef
1/2 tsp (1 g) ground cumin
1/8 tsp (.33 g) ground clove
1/8 tsp (.33 g) ground cinnamon
1 tsp (5 g) salt
1/2 tsp (1 g) black pepper

1. Remove the stems and seeds from the dried guajillo chiles. Rinse well, place into a small pot with water covering the chiles and bring to a boil. Boil for 1 minute, turn off the heat, cover and steep for at least 30 minutes or until the chiles are softened.

2. Remove the chiles from soaking liquid and place in a blender. Add garlic, dried bay leaf, Mexican oregano, apple cider vinegar and water. Then puree well.

3. In the bowl of ground meat, add puree, ground cumin, ground clove, ground cinnamon, black pepper and salt. Mix well for at least 5 minutes.

4. Place chorizo mixture in a glass storage bowl with a lid, and place in the refrigerator to marinate overnight. You can also freeze this for up to 8 weeks.

5. To cook, preheat a large skillet over a medium heat, add 2 Tbsp cooking oil and half of the marinated chorizo. Start breaking up the meat and cooking. Once the chorizo is browned and cooked, add 6 large beaten eggs, combine and cook with chorizo until desired doneness and serve.

NOTES: If liquid has collected at the bottom of the bowl after marinating, drain it before cooking. After marinating, you can divide the chorizo into your preferred amounts and store in a freezer-safe storage bag or container for up to 8 weeks. Be sure to completely thaw and drain extra liquid before cooking.

POP'S FIDEO CON POLLO

2 tsp (10 g) salt
2 tsp (6 g) paprika
2 tsp (8 g) onion powder
2 tsp (8 g) garlic powder
2 tsp (8 g) salt-free lemon pepper
3 lbs (1.36 kg) bone in chicken thighs or legs
1 medium zucchini (195 g)
1 medium carrot (60 g)
1 large potato (300 g)
10 oz (282 g) vermicelli pasta
1/4 tsp (1.25 g) salt
1/2 medium onion (90 g)
2 cloves garlic (8 g) minced
6 cups (1.42 L) water
2 Tbsp (20 g) chicken bouillon powder
9.1 oz (260 g) crushed tomatoes
1/2 (1.5 g) ground cumin
1/2 tsp (1 g) black pepper

1. In a small bowl, combine salt, paprika, onion powder, garlic powder and lemon pepper.

2. Using the seasoning mix, season the chicken thighs on both sides.

3. To prepare the vegetables, chop zucchini, carrot, potato and onion into large chunks.

4. In a preheated large wide pot with a lid, add 3 Tbsp cooking oil and arrange the chicken skin side down. Using a medium high heat, brown the chicken for 5 minutes on each side. If needed, do this in several batches to avoid a crowded pot.

5. Once the chicken is browned, remove from the pot and set aside until ready to use. Allow any juices to simmer away and leave any rendered fat in the pot.

CONTINUE TO PAGE 46

6. Lower the heat to a low setting. To the same pot, add vermicelli pasta and toast for 7 to 8 minutes or until golden brown.

7. To the toasted pasta, add chopped carrots, potatoes and 1/4 tsp salt. Then sauté for 3 minutes. Then add in minced garlic and continue to sauté for an additional minute.

8. Now add water, bouillon powder, crushed tomatoes, ground cumin and black pepper.

9. Place the chicken back into the pot, add large chunks of onions and bring to a rapid simmer.

10. Cover with a lid, lower the heat and gently simmer for 20 to 22 minutes.

11. After cooking time, do not lift the lid. Turn off the heat, let sit for 5 minutes, then serve.

NOTES: Be sure to toast the pasta well. This will ensure that the texture of the pasta does not turn mushy and bloated after the cook time. This makes at least 4 to 6 servings.

SIMPLE SLOW COOKER PORK SHOULDER

4 lbs (1.81 kg) boneless pork shoulder roast
2 1/2 (12 g) salt
1 tsp (2 g) black pepper
1 small onion (100 g)
4 cloves garlic (16 g)
2 cups (473 ml) low sodium chicken broth
1 dried bay leaf

1. In a 4.5 quart slow cooker, add all of the ingredients.

2. Place the lid on the slow cooker, set to low setting and cook for 8 to 10 hours. If using a high setting, then cook for 6 to 8 hours or until the pork is cooked and tender.

NOTES: You can salt and season to your preference. This recipe is perfect to chop and use as a meat filling option for tamales. After removing the meat, any juice, broth or rendered fat left in the slow cooker can be used for the masa dough when making tamales.

SIMPLE SLOW COOKER BEEF CHUCK ROAST

4 lbs (1.81 kg) boneless chuck roast beef
2 1/2 (12 g) salt
1 tsp (2 g) black pepper
1 small onion (100 g)
4 cloves garlic (16 g)
2 cups (473 ml) low sodium beef broth
1 dried bay leaf

1. In a 4.5 quart slow cooker, add all of the ingredients.
2. Place the lid on the slow cooker, set to low setting and cook for 8 to 10 hours. If using high setting, then cook for 6 to 8 hours or until the beef is cooked and tender.

NOTES: You can salt and season to your preference. This recipe is perfect to chop and use as a meat option for tamales. After removing the meat, any juice, broth or rendered fat left in the slow cooker can be used for the masa dough when making tamales.

SIMPLE SLOW COOKER BEEF BARBACOA

3 lbs (1.36 kg) beef cheeks or beef shanks
2 tsp (10 g) salt
2 dried bay leaves
4 cloves garlic (16 g)
1/2 tsp (1 g) black pepper
4.5 quart slow cooker

1. In a 4.5 quart slow cooker, add the beef cheeks, salt, dried bay leaves, garlic and black pepper.
2. Place the lid on the slow cooker, set to the low setting and cook for 11 to 12 hours or cook on high setting for 7 to 8 hours.
3. When the meat is soft and tender, remove meat onto a plate.
4. Shred only when ready to serve.

NOTES: No liquid is needed in this recipe as the meat will render its natural juices and fat. The 3 lbs of meat will yield close to 1 1/2 lbs to 2 lbs of barbacoa depending on the fat ratio of the cut of beef. Shred the meat only when you serve and eat. This will help retain the moisture of the meat longer.

CHEESY BEEF CORNBREAD TAMALE PIE

2 Tbsp (30 ml) cooking oil
1 lb (454 g) lean ground beef
1 Tbsp (10 g) beef bouillon powder
2 Tbsp chili powder
1 tsp (4 g) garlic powder
1 tsp (4 g) onion powder
½ tsp (1.5 g) ground cumin
2 Tbsp (20 g) all-purpose flour
8 fl oz (236.5 ml) water
1 ¼ cups (125 g) cheddar cheese shredded
2 Tbsp (28.5 g) unsalted butter softened
jalapeño cornbread batter
(see recipe for Mama's Jalapeño Cheese Cornbread)

1. In a preheated skillet, add cooking oil, ground beef and cook through.

2. Next add beef bouillon powder, chili powder, garlic powder, onion powder, ground cumin, all-purpose four and combine well with cooked ground beef.

3. Now add water, combine until smooth and simmer until thick gravy forms. Then set aside until needed.

4. Combine and mix all of the ingredients for jalapeño cornbread batter. See recipe.

5. Butter an 8x12 inch baking dish with the 2 Tbsp of softened butter.

6. Now pour half of the cornbread batter at the bottom of the baking dish. Add all of the ground beef mixture. Layer the shredded cheese and top with the remainder of cornbread batter.

7. Bake in a preheated oven at 400 °F / 204 °C for 22 to 25 minutes.

8. Remove from the oven, rest for 10 minutes and serve.

NOTES: This makes at least 6 to 8 servings. Garnish with sour cream and scallions.

MAMA'S JALAPEÑO CHEESE CORNBREAD

1 cup (130 g) yellow corn meal
1/2 cup (65 g) all purpose flour
1 Tbsp (15 g) baking powder
1/2 tsp (2.5 g) salt
2 Tbsp (25 g) granulated sugar
1 large egg
½ cup (118 ml) whole milk
1 Tbsp (15 ml) cooking oil
¾ cup (180 g) canned cream corn
4 oz (112 g) shredded cheddar cheese
1 scallion (26g) chopped
2 oz (52 g) pickled jalapeños chopped
3 Tbsp (42 g) unsalted butter (softened)

1. In a bowl, combine corn meal, flour, baking powder, salt and sugar.

2. Add milk, egg, cooking oil, cream corn and combine well.

3. Now fold in shredded cheese, scallions, and pickled jalapeños.

4. In an 8 inch baking pan or cast iron skillet, add softened butter to coat the skillet. Now pour in corn bread batter.

5. Bake in a preheated oven at 400 °F / 204 °C for 23 to 25 minutes or until cooked through.

NOTES: You can also use an 8 inch cake pan or square baking dish. This makes 8 servings.

SIMPLE OVEN BAKED BBQ CHICKEN

1 1/2 tsp (6 g) garlic powder

1 1/2 tsp (6 g) onion powder

1 1/2 tsp (5 g) smoked paprika

1 1/2 tsp (6 g) salt-free lemon pepper

1 1/2 tsp (7.5 g) salt

3 lbs (1.36 kg) bone in chicken legs or thighs

BBQ SAUCE

1 cup (236.5) ketchup

1 1/2 tbsp (22.5 ml) soy sauce

1 Tbsp (15 ml) apple cider vinegar

1/4 cup (85 g) honey

1 1/2 tsp (7.5 g) reserved dry seasoning mix

1. In a small bowl, combine garlic powder, onion powder, smoked paprika, lemon pepper and salt. Once seasoning is mixed, reserve 1 1/2 tsp in a separate small dish and set aside for later use.

2. With the remaining dry seasoning mix, season the chicken all over and place on a baking sheet lined with parchment paper. Be sure to leave space between the pieces of chicken to ensure even cooking.

3. Bake the chicken in a preheated oven at 375 °F / 190 °C for 45 to 50 minutes.

4. In a small pan over a low heat, add ketchup, soy sauce, apple cider vinegar, honey and reserved dry seasoning mix. Then combine well.

5. Stir and simmer sauce for five minutes. Then set aside until needed.

6. Remove the chicken from the oven and baste each piece of chicken with a generous amount of sauce.

7. Place the oven on a broil setting, return the sauced chicken to the oven and broil for 3 minutes or until the exterior of the sauced chicken starts to simmer and slightly char.

8. Remove from the oven, rest for 5 minutes and serve.

NOTES: To ensure even cooked chicken, be sure to completely thaw and cook until the internal temperature reaches 165 °F / 74 °C. This makes at least 4 servings.

MAMA'S FAVORITE BBQ SPICE RUB

3/4 packed cup (148.5 g) dark brown sugar
4 Tbsp (32 g) dried minced onion
4 Tbsp (40 g)beef bouillon powder
3 Tbsp (21 g) chili powder
3 Tbsp (16 g) smoked paprika
1 Tbsp (9 g) smoked sea salt
3 Tbsp (20 g) salt free lemon pepper
3 Tbsp (27 g) garlic powder

1. In a cleaned dry bowl, add all ingredients and mix well.
2. Store in a cleaned dry jar or container with a lid.

NOTES: This rub is great for seasoning slow cooked or baked ribs, steaks and chicken.

HOMESTYLE KOREAN FRIED CHICKEN

1/2 tsp (1 g) ground ginger powder
1/2 tsp (1 g) fine Korean red pepper powder
1 tsp (4 g) garlic powder
1 tsp (4 g) onion powder
1/2 tsp (2.5 g) salt
2 to 2 1/2 lbs (1 to 1 1/2 kg) flats and drumettes of chicken wings
1/4 cup (60 ml) rice wine or buttermilk

BATTER
1/2 cup (65 g) potato starch (or cornstarch)
1/2 cup (65 g) all purpose flour
1/2 tsp (2.5 g) salt
1/2 tsp (2.5 g) sugar
1/2 tsp (1 g) ground ginger powder
1/2 tsp (1 g) fine Korean red pepper powder
1 tsp (4 g) granulated garlic powder
1 tsp (4 g) granulated onion powder
5 fl oz (145 ml) cold water

1. In a small bowl, combine ground ginger powder, red pepper powder, garlic powder, onion powder and salt.

2. In a large bowl, add the chicken, rice wine and seasoning mix. Combine, cover, and place in the refrigerator. Marinate for at least 2 hours.

3. In a large bowl, combine potato starch, flour, salt, sugar, ground ginger powder, red pepper powder, garlic powder and onion powder. Add cold water, and combine well.

4. Remove the chicken from the marinade and place in the batter. Mix and coat the chicken well.

5. In a deep frying pan or pot, add at least 1 inch deep of cooking oil. Preheat to 350 °F / 176 °C.

CONTINUE TO PAGE 56

6. Place single pieces of battered chicken into the fry oil. Fry in batches to avoid crowding the pan. Fry the chicken for 3 minutes, then remove from oil and place on a baking sheet with a rack.

7. After the first fry, allow the fry oil to reach 350 °F / 176 °C. Then fry the chicken for a second time in batches for 3 to 5 additional minutes.

8. Place double fry chicken back on the baking sheet with a rack to allow any residual oil to run off. Then serve.

NOTES: To ensure even cooked chicken, be sure to completely thaw and cook until the internal temperature reaches 165 °F / 74 °C. This makes 1 to 2 servings.

SOUPS
& STEWS

EASY SLOW COOKER BEEF BIRRIA

3 guajillo chiles (18 g)

1 ancho chile (18 g)

1 pasilla chile (12 g)

6 cloves of garlic (24 g)

1 chipotle pepper in adobo sauce (optional)

1 tsp (1 g) Mexican oregano

3 lbs (1.36 kg) beef shanks

1 small onion (100 g)

1 1/2 tsp (7.5 g) salt

2 Tbsp (20 g) beef bouillon powder

1 tsp (2 g) black pepper

1/8 tsp (.33 g) ground clove

1/8 tsp (.33 g) ground cinnamon

1 Tbsp (3 g) fresh thyme

2 dried bay leaves

5 cups (1.18 L) water

1. Remove the stems and seeds from guajillo, ancho and pasilla chiles. Rinse and wash well to remove any debris.

2. Add the cleaned chiles to a small pot of water, bring to a boil, turn off heat, cover with a lid and steep for 30 minutes or until softened.

3. Remove the chiles from the pot and discard soaking liquid. Add softened chiles, garlic, Mexican oregano, chipotle pepper and 1 cup of water to a blender. Blend until pureed well. Set aside until ready to use.

4. In a preheated large skillet, add 3 Tbsp cooking oil and brown the beef shanks on each side for 2 minutes on a medium heat. Then remove from the pan and place all the browned beef into a 4.5 quart slow cooker.

5. Dice the onion and add to the slow cooker along with chile puree, salt, beef bouillon powder, black pepper, ground cloves, ground cinnamon and fresh thyme. Then combine well.

6. Pour in the remaining 4 cups of the water, add the dried bay leaves and cover with a lid. Cook for 6 to 8 hours on the low setting or cook for 4 to 6 hours on the high setting.

7. Once the cooking time is up, skim out all of the rendered fat, stir the beef birria and shred some of the meat. Serve in a bowl or use for tacos.

NOTES: You can salt and season to your preference. You can garnish your bowl with fresh onion, cilantro and a squeeze of lime. This makes at least 4 to 6 servings.

EASY MENUDO WITH HOMINY

5 lbs (2.67 kg) honeycomb beef tripe
9 to 10 quarts (8.5 to 9.5 L) water
3 cloves garlic (12 g)
2 dried bay leaves
1/2 medium onion (85 g)
30 oz (850 g) can of hominy
salt to taste

MENUDO SPICE MIX

8 Tbsp (57 g) chili powder
1 Tbsp (8.5 g) onion powder
1 Tbsp (8.5 g) garlic powder
2 tsp (5 g) ground cumin
1 Tbsp (2 g) Mexican oregano
2 Tbsp (20 g) beef or chicken bouillon powder

1. In a bowl, add chili powder, onion powder, garlic powder, and ground cumin, Mexican oregano and bouillon powder. Then combine well.

2. Wash and rinse the beef tripe well. Then cut in to bite size pieces.

3. Using a 12 quart pot, add 9 quarts of water, beef tripe, whole garlic, dried bay leaves and onion.

4. Bring water to a boil and then cook uncovered for 1 hour. Try to keep the water between a rapid simmer to rolling boil. Adjust heat source accordingly. Be sure to skim any foam throughout the cook time.

5. Next add the menudo spice mix, stir and continue to rapidly simmer. You will need to taste and add salt to preference. Start by adding 2 tsp to 1 Tbsp of salt, mix and taste. Cook and rapidly simmer for another 30 minutes.

6. Drain and rinse the can of hominy. Add to the pot of menudo and continue cooking for another 15 to 20 minutes or until the beef tripe is tender. Taste the menudo for seasoning or salt and adjust to your preference, then serve.

NOTES: The bouillon powder used in the spice mix can be substituted for 1 Tbsp of salt. This makes at least 8 servings. Garnish with fresh diced jalapeño, cilantro, onion and a squeeze of lime.

EASY RED PORK POZOLE

5 lbs (2.27 kg) boneless pork shoulder roast
6 quarts (5.68 L) water
2 1/2 tsp (12 g) salt
2 bay leaves
4 dried ancho chiles (45 g)
5 dried guajillo chiles (30 g)
1/2 medium onion (85 g)
5 cloves of garlic (20 g)
2 Tbsp (20 g) chicken bouillon powder
2 tsp (6 g) ground cumin
1 Tbsp (2 g) dried Mexican oregano
2 cans (30 oz each) (1.7 kg) hominy

1. Cut the pork meat into large chunks.

2. Using a 10 quart pot, add water, pork meat, salt and dried bay leaves. Bring to a boil.

3. Once the water is rapidly simmering, cook uncovered for 1 hour. Try to keep the water between a rapid simmer to a rolling boil. Adjust the heat source accordingly. Be sure to skim any foam throughout the cook time.

4. For the puree, remove the stems and seeds from guajillo and ancho chiles. Rinse and wash well to remove any debris.

5. Add the cleaned chiles to a small pot of water, bring to a boil, turn off heat, cover with a lid and steep for 30 minutes or until softened.

6. After 1 hour of cooking time, collect 2 cups of boiling broth from the pot of boiled pork meat into a measuring cup and set aside until needed.

7. Remove the chiles from the small pot and discard the soaking liquid. Add the softened chiles, onion, garlic, Mexican oregano and 2 cups of reserved broth to a blender. Puree well and strain through a fine wire mesh strainer.

8. After an hour of cooking time, add chili puree to a pot of boiling pork meat, chicken bouillon powder and ground cumin. Stir, cover with a lid, and continue to cook for 20 minutes.

9. Remove most of the pork meat and break apart into smaller chunks of meat. You can also shred some of the pork for added texture to the soup. Add meat back into the pot and stir.

10. Drain and rinse both cans of hominy. Add the hominy to the pot, stir and continue cooking for an additional 15 to 20 minutes. Taste soup for salt and seasoning, then adjust to your preference and taste.

11. Serve with garnishes of thinly sliced cherry radishes, diced onion, thinly shredded fresh cabbage and a squeeze of fresh lime.

NOTES: This makes at least 6 to 8 servings.

EASY RED CHICKEN POZOLE

6 quarts (5.68 L) water
5 lbs (2.27 kg) bone in chicken pieces
2 bay leaves
2 1/2 tsp (12 g) salt
4 dried ancho chiles (45 g)
5 dried guajillo chiles (30 g)
1/2 medium onion (85 g)
5 cloves of garlic (20 g)
2 Tbsp (20 g) chicken bouillon powder
2 tsp (6 g) ground cumin
1 Tbsp (2 g) dried Mexican oregano
2 cans (30 oz each) (1.7 kg) hominy

1. Using a 10 quart pot, add 5 quarts of water, chicken, dried bay leaves and salt. Bring to a boil.

2. Once water is rapidly simmering, cook uncovered for 45 minutes to an hour. Try to keep the water between a rapid simmer to gentle simmer. Adjust the heat source accordingly. Be sure to skim any foam throughout the cook time.

3. Remove the stems and seeds from the guajillo and ancho chiles. Rinse and wash well to remove any debris.

4. Add cleaned chiles to a small pot of water. Bring to a boil, turn off heat, cover with a lid and steep for 30 minutes or until softened.

5. After 45 minutes of cooking time, reserve 2 cups of boiling broth from the pot of chicken and set aside until needed.

6. Remove the chiles from the pot and discard soaking liquid. Add the softened chiles, onion, garlic, Mexican oregano and the 2 cups of reserved broth to a blender. Puree well and strain through a fine wire mesh strainer.

7. Now add chili puree, ground cumin and chicken bouillon powder to the pot of simmering chicken. Stir, cover with a lid and continue to cook for 20 minutes.

8. Drain and rinse both cans of hominy. Add the hominy to the pot, stir and continue cooking for an additional 15 to 20 minutes. Taste for salt and seasoning, then adjust to your preference and taste.

9. Serve with garnishes of thinly sliced cherry radishes, diced onion, thinly shredded fresh cabbage and a squeeze of fresh lime.

NOTES: You can serve this soup using pieces of the chicken or shred the tender chicken meat and add back to the pot. This makes at least 6 to 8 servings.

EASY CHICKEN POZOLE VERDE

5 quarts (3.8 L) water
3lbs (1.36 kg) bone-in chicken thighs
1 medium onion (170 g)
4 cloves garlic (16 g)
2 dried bay leaves
1 lb (454 g) tomatillos
2 fresh poblano peppers
2 Tbsp (20 g) chicken bouillon powder
1/3 cup (and 50 g) toasted pumpkin seeds
handful (15 g) fresh cilantro
2 cups (60 g) fresh baby spinach leaves
1 Tbsp (2 g) Mexican oregano
2 cans (30 oz each) (1.7 kg) hominy

1. Using an 8 to 10 quart pot, add 5 quarts of water, chicken, onion, garlic, dried bay leaves and salt. Bring to a boil.

2. Once water is rapidly simmering, cook uncovered for 40 minutes. Try to keep the water between a rapid simmer to gentle simmer. Adjust the heat source accordingly. Be sure to skim any foam throughout the cook time.

3. Once the chicken is cooked, remove from pot, shred and set aside until needed.

4. Strain the pot of broth, pour strained broth back into the pot and set aside until needed. Discard bay leaves and save any cooked ingredients left in the strainer from the broth.

5. To prepare for the puree, remove husks from tomatillos, rinse and slice in half. Char the poblano peppers on an open flame, place in a glass bowl, cover with cling film and set for 15 minutes. Wipe off charred skins with a damp paper towel, remove stems, seeds and rinse well.

6. In a blender, add the poblano peppers, tomatillos, reserved onion and garlic from the strained broth, toasted pumpkin seeds, handful of fresh cilantro, handful of fresh spinach, Mexican oregano and 2 cups of reserved broth. Puree well.

7. Drain and rinse hominy.

8. Bring the pot of reserved broth back to a rapid simmer then add hominy, puree and chicken bouillon powder. Simmer for 20 minutes.

9. Add the reserved shredded chicken into the pot, stir and cook for an additional 10 minutes.

10. Serve with garnishes of thinly sliced cherry radishes, diced onion, thinly shredded fresh cabbage and a squeeze of fresh lime.

NOTES: You can serve this soup using pieces of the chicken or shred the tender chicken meat and add back to the pot. This makes at least 6 to 8 servings.

MEXICAN STYLE CHICKEN SOUP

3 quarts (2.8 L) water
2 1/2 lbs (1.13 kg) bone-in chicken pieces
1 medium onion (170 g)
4 cloves garlic (16 g)
1 dried bay leaves
2 tsp (10 g) salt
1/2 tsp (1 g) black pepper
3 medium potatoes (360 g)
1 chayote (245 g)
1 celery stick (55 g)
1 lb (454 g) cabbage
2 ears of fresh corn (385 g)
2 medium Mexican squash (400 g)
2 Tbsp (20 g) chicken bouillon powder

1. Using a 6 to 8 quart pot, add water, chicken, chopped onion, minced garlic, dried bay leaves, salt and pepper. Bring to a boil.

2. Once the water is rapidly simmering, cook uncovered for 30 minutes. Try to keep the water between a rapid simmer to a gentle simmer. Adjust the heat source accordingly. Be sure to skim any foam throughout the cook time.

3. Prepare all fresh vegetables and cut into large chunks or pieces. The corn can be cut into smaller pieces.

4. To the pot, add the potatoes, carrot, celery and chayote. Once the pot is rapidly simmering again, cover with a lid and continue to cook for 15 minutes or until the carrots and potatoes are knife tender.

5. Next add chicken bouillon powder and stir until combined.

6. Now add the large chunks of squash, corn and chopped cabbage. Bring back to a rapid simmer, cover with a lid and continue cooking for 15 minutes or until cabbage and squash reach desired doneness.

7. Taste the broth and adjust salt or seasoning to your preference. Once the soup is done then serve.

NOTES: You can serve this soup using pieces of the chicken or shred the tender chicken meat and add back to the pot. Add fresh squeezed lime to soup for added flavor. This makes at least 6 to 8 servings.

MEXICAN STYLE BEEF SOUP

4 1/2 quarts (3.78 L) water
3 lbs (1.36 kg) beef shanks
1 medium onion (170 g)
4 cloves garlic (16 g)
1 dried bay leaves
1 Tbsp (11.25 g) salt
1 tsp (2 g) black pepper
3 medium potatoes (360 g)
1 chayote (245 g)
1 celery stick (55 g)
1 lb (454 g) cabbage
2 ears of fresh corn (385 g)
2 medium Mexican squash (400 g)
2 Tbsp (20 g) beef bouillon powder

1. Using an 8 quart pot, add water, beef shanks, chopped onion, minced garlic, dried bay leaves, salt and pepper. Bring to a boil.

2. Once water is rapidly simmering, cook uncovered for 1 hour. Try to keep the water between a rapid simmer to gentle simmer. Adjust the heat source accordingly. Be sure to skim any foam throughout the cook time.

3. Prepare all of the fresh vegetables and cut into large chunks or pieces. The corn can be cut into smaller pieces.

4. To the pot, add the potatoes, carrot, celery and chayote. Once the pot is rapidly simmering again, cover with a lid and continue to cook for 15 minutes or until carrots and potatoes are knife tender.

5. Next add beef bouillon powder and stir until combined.

6. Now add the large chunks of squash, corn and chopped cabbage. Bring back to a rapid simmer, cover with a lid and continue cooking for 15 minutes or until cabbage and squash reach desired doneness.

7. Taste broth and adjust salt or seasoning to your preference. Once soup is done then serve.

NOTES: You can serve this soup using pieces of the chicken or shred the tender chicken meat and add back to the pot. Add fresh squeezed lime to soup for added flavor. This makes at least 6 servings.

MEXICAN STYLE PORK WITH SQUASH

1 tsp (5 g) salt
1/2 tsp (1 g) black pepper
1/2 tsp (2 g) onion powder
1/2 tsp (2 g) garlic powder
1/2 tsp (1.5 g) ground cumin
2 1/2 lbs (1.13 kg) cubed boneless pork loin or pork shoulder meat
1 small onion (120 g)
3 cloves of garlic minced (12 g)
kernels from 2 ears of fresh sweet corn (295 g)
1/2 tsp (1 g) Mexican oregano
1 1/2 cup (350 mL) low sodium chicken broth
2/3 cup (190 g) crushed tomato
4 medium Mexican squash (860 g)
1 large jalapeño (optional)
a bunch of fresh cilantro (optional)

1. In a small bowl, add salt, pepper, ground cumin, onion powder and garlic powder. Then combine.

2. Cut the pork meat into bite sized cubes and season with seasoning mixture.

3. In a preheated wide bottom pot or dutch oven, add 3 Tbsp cooking oil and brown half of the pork meat over a medium high heat. Remove from the pot, set aside and repeat the process for the other half of pork meat. Set browned pork meat aside until needed.

4. In the same pot, lower the heat to a medium setting, add 1 Tbsp cooking oil if needed, then add diced onion and a pinch of salt. Sauté until onion is softened. Then add minced garlic, fresh corn kernels, another pinch of salt and Mexican oregano. Continue to sauté for 2 minutes.

5. Now add low sodium chicken broth, stir and scrape any fond at the bottom surface of the pot. Add crushed tomato, mix and combine well.

6. Once the liquid is at a gentle simmer, add the browned pork meat and chopped Mexican squash. Combine well. Place the whole jalapeño and fresh bunch of cilantro on top. Bring to a simmer, cover with a lid, lower the heat and cook for 23 to 25 minutes.

7. After cooking, turn off the heat, uncover and serve.

NOTES: This makes at least 6 servings.

RICE, BEANS & SIDES

EASY MEXICAN STYLE RICE

1 cup (160 g) long grain rice
1/2 small onion (80 g)
2 cloves garlic minced (13 g)
2 cups (473 ml) water
1 Tbsp (10 g) chicken bouillon powder
1/2 cup (120 ml) tomato sauce
1/2 tsp (1.5 g) ground cumin
1/2 tsp (1g) black pepper

1. Rinse and drain the rice. Set aside in a fine mesh strainer until ready to use.

2. To a preheated pan, add 3 Tbsp cooking oil and the rice. Toast for 5 minutes or until golden brown using a medium low heat.

3. Next add diced onion and minced garlic to the rice, and sauté for 1 minute.

4. Combine water and chicken bouillon powder, then pour into the skillet with toasted rice.

5. Next add tomato sauce, ground cumin and black pepper. Then combine.

6. Bring to a gentle boil, cover with a lid, set the heat to a low setting and simmer for 18 to 20 minutes.

7. After the cook time, turn off the heat. DO NOT lift the lid and allow it to set covered for 5 to 10 minutes.

8. Then uncover, fluff and serve.

NOTES: You can substitute the chicken bouillon powder and water with chicken broth or stock and salt to your preference. It is important to allow the rice to set after the cook time. The rice will continue to cook with the residual heat and absorb any liquid left in the pan. This makes 4 to 6 servings.

SIMPLE CHARRO BEANS

1 lb (454 g) dried pinto beans
4 1/2 quarts (4.25 L) water
2 cloves garlic minced (13 g)
1 large onion (265 g)
5 cloves garlic (20 g)
1 large jalapeño (50 g)
12 oz (340 g) smoked bacon
3 Roma tomatoes (260 g)
1 handful cilantro (15 g)
1 Tbsp (10 g) chicken bouillon powder
2 tsp (10 g) salt

1. Rinse and clean the dried pinto beans. Soak in 1 1/2 quarts of water overnight.

2. Drain the beans from soaking water and add to a large pot. Add 4 1/2 quarts water to the pot, bring to a boil and cook for 1 hour at a low boil.

3. Dice onion, mince garlic and chop tomatoes. Remove the stem and seeds from jalapeño, then dice. Chop the bacon and set aside until ready to use.

4. In a cold pan, add the chopped bacon, turn on the heat to a medium setting and cook the bacon. Once cooked, remove the bacon from the rendered fat and set on a plate lined with a paper towel.

5. Remove most of the rendered fat from the pan leaving 2 Tbsp of bacon fat. On a medium heat, sauté the onions, tomatoes, garlic and jalapeño for 3 minutes.

6. After the beans have cooked for one hour, add sauté of vegetables from pan, cooked bacon, chicken bouillon powder and salt. Then mix well. Once the beans come to a rapid simmer, cover with a lid and continue to cook until beans are tender. Taste for salt and adjust to your preference.

NOTES: This makes at least 8 to 10 servings.

EASY HOMEMADE YELLOW RICE

1 cup (160 g) long grain rice
3 Tbsp (45 ml) cooking oil
1/3 cup (40 g) onion
3 Tbsp (30 g) yellow bell pepper
2 cloves garlic (8 g)
1 Tbsp (10 g) chicken bouillon powder
1/4 tsp (.5 g) ground turmeric
1/4 tsp (1 g) garlic powder
1/4 tsp (1 g) onion powder
2 cups (473 ml) water

1. Rinse and drain the rice. Set aside in a fine mesh strainer until ready to use.

2. To a preheated pan, add 3 Tbsp cooking oil and the rice. Toast for 5 minutes or until golden brown using a medium to medium low heat. Cook time will vary.

3. Next add finely minced onion and bell pepper to the rice. Sauté for 2 minutes. Then add garlic and sauté for another minute.

4. Combine ground turmeric, garlic powder, onion powder and chicken bouillon powder. Quickly mix into rice.

5. Add water, bring to a gentle boil, cover with a lid, set the heat to a low setting and simmer for 18 to 20 minutes.

6. After the cook time, turn off the heat. DO NOT lift the lid and allow it to set covered for 5 to 10 minutes.

7. Then uncover, fluff and serve.

NOTES: You can substitute the chicken bouillon powder and water with chicken broth. You may need to and salt to taste. It is important to allow the rice to set after the cook time. The rice will continue to cook with the residual heat and absorb any liquid left in the pan. This makes 4 to 6 servings.

ZESTY CILANTRO LIME RICE

1 cup (160 g) long grain rice
2 Tbsp (30 ml) cooking oil
1/3 cup (40 g) onion
2 cloves garlic (8 g)
1 Tbsp (10 g) chicken bouillon powder
zest of large lime
2 cups (473 ml) water
3 Tbsp (45 ml) fresh squeezed lime juice
4 cilantro stems (5 g)
1/4 cup (10 g) chopped fresh cilantro leaves

1. Rinse and drain the rice. Set aside in a fine mesh strainer until ready to use.

2. To a preheated pan, add cooking oil and the rice. Toast for 5 minutes or until golden brown using a medium to medium low heat. Cook time will vary.

3. Next add finely minced onion and sauté for 2 minute. Then add garlic and sauté for another minute.

4. Add chicken bouillon powder and lime zest, then quickly mix in toasted rice.

5. Add water, lime juice and bundled cilantro stems. Then bring to a gentle boil, cover with a lid, set the heat to a low setting and simmer for 18 to 20 minutes.

6. After the cook time, turn off the heat. DO NOT lift the lid and allow it to set covered for 5 to 10 minutes.

7. Uncover, remove cilantro stems, add chopped fresh cilantro leaves, fluff and serve.

NOTES: You can substitute the chicken bouillon powder and water with chicken broth. You may need to and salt to taste. It is important to allow the rice to set after the cook time. The rice will continue to cook with the residual heat and absorb any liquid left in the pan. This makes 4 to 6 servings.

CREAMY STOVETOP MAC AND CHEESE

2 Tbsp butter
1/4 tsp (.5 g) paprika
1/4 tsp (1 g) onion powder
1/4 tsp (1.25 g) salt (optional)
8 oz (226 g) softened cream cheese
12 oz (354.88 ml) half cream and half whole milk
8 oz (226 g) shredded mild cheddar cheese
1 lb (454 g) elbow macaroni

1. In a preheated sauce pot on a medium low heat, add butter, Korean red pepper powder and onion powder. Then heat for 30 seconds.

2. Now add softened cream cheese and whisk until completely melted and creamy.

3. Add half and half and combine well.

4. Add shredded cheddar cheese, stir and combine until cheese sauce is smooth and creamy. Remove from the heat or turn heat to the lowest setting until ready to use.

5. In a pot of 2 1/2 to 3 quarts of boiling water add 2 Tbsp salt, mix and add elbow macaroni. Stir and bring water back up to rolling boil then cook for 10 minutes or until desired doneness.

6. Drain water from the elbow macaroni. Now combine the elbow macaroni and cheese sauce. Mix well and serve.

NOTES: You can substitute the 8 oz of cream cheese for mascarpone cheese. This makes at least 6 to 8 servings.

CREAMY SPICY MAC AND CHEESE

2 Tbsp butter
1/2 tsp (2 g) Korean red pepper powder
1/4 tsp (1 g) onion powder
1/4 tsp (1.25 g) salt (optional)
8 oz (226 g) softened cream cheese
12 oz (354.88 ml) half cream and half whole milk
8 oz (226 g) shredded mild cheddar cheese
2 Tbsp Korean Buldak sauce
1 lb (454 g) elbow macaroni

1. In a preheated sauce pot on a medium low heat, add butter, Korean red pepper powder and onion powder. Then heat for 30 seconds.

2. Now add softened cream cheese and whisk until completely melted and creamy.

3. Add half and half and combine well.

4. Add shredded cheddar cheese, stir and combine until cheese sauce is smooth and creamy. Then add and mix in Buldak sauce. Remove from heat or turn heat to lowest setting until ready to use.

5. In a pot of 2 1/2 to 3 quarts of boiling water, add 2 Tbsp salt, mix and add elbow macaroni. Stir and bring water back up to rolling boil then cook for 10 minutes or until desired doneness.

6. Drain water from the elbow macaroni. Now combine the elbow macaroni and cheese sauce. Mix well and serve.

NOTES: You can substitute the 8 oz of cream cheese for mascarpone cheese. The Korean red pepper powder can be substituted with 1/4 tsp cayenne powder. Buldak sauce is a Korean spicy chicken flavored fire noodle sauce with a hint of smoky flavor. This makes at least 6 to 8 servings.

SIMPLE AND EASY COLESLAW

1 cup (237 ml) whole milk
3 /4 cup (155 g) mayonnaise
1 1/2 Tbsp (13 ml) fresh lemon juice
1 Tbsp (15 g) finely minced onion
2 Tbsp (20 g) sugar
1 1/2 tsp (8 g) salt
1/4 tsp (1 g) black pepper
1 1/2 lbs (681 g) shredded chopped cabbage
1 shredded medium to large carrot (75 g)

1. For the dressing, in a bowl, add whole milk, mayonnaise, fresh lemon juice, finely minced onion, sugar, salt and black pepper. Then combine well.

2. In a separate large bowl, add shredded cabbage, shredded carrot and dressing. Combine well.

3. Cover, refrigerate and allow to set for at least 2 to 3 hours, overnight for best results.

NOTES: This makes at least 8 servings.

SWEETS &
BAKED TREATS

ABUELITA'S ARROZ CON LECHE

4 cups (960 ml) water
1 medium cinnamon stick
2 whole cloves
1/2 cup (80 g) long grain rice
12 oz can evaporated milk (354 ml)
4 Tbsp (52 g) sugar
1/4 tsp (1.25 g) salt

1. In a pot, add water, cinnamon stick and cloves. Bring to a simmer, cover with a lid and gently simmer for 15 minutes.

2. Rinse and drain the rice in cold water. Then add to the pot of simmering liquid.

3. Bring back to a simmer, cover with a lid and gently simmer for 20 minutes.

4. Now add evaporated milk, sugar and a pinch of salt. Mix and combine well.

5. Gently simmer for 10 minutes.

6. Turn off heat, set for 10 minutes, mix and serve.

NOTES: This makes at least 4 servings.

BO'S SUNFLOWER BUTTER CHOCOLATE PIE

1 cup (236.5 g) heavy cream
1 cup (236.5 g) whole milk
3.4 oz (96 g) package instant vanilla pudding
1 ready-made 9 inch shortbread crust
1/2 cup (125 g) seed or nut butter of choice
***garnish* roasted sunflower seeds (or nuts of choice)**

GANACHE
5 oz (141 g) semi-sweet chocolate chips
1/4 cup (60 ml) heavy cream

1. Add heavy cream in a heat proof cup and microwave in 15 second intervals until hot.

2. Roughly chop the chocolate chips, put in a small bowl, pour over heated heavy cream and set for ten minutes without stirring.

3. After ten minutes, stir and combine into a smooth creamy chocolate sauce.

4. In a chilled large bowl, add heavy cream, whole milk and instant vanilla pudding. Whisk until well combined. Now fold in and combine the sunflower butter until mixed well.

5. Pour the pudding mixture into the pie shell and smooth over the surface.

6. Now pour over the ganache and smooth over the surface.

7. Chop the roasted seeds and garnish around the top edge of the pie.

8. Refrigerate the pie for at least 4 hours to set. Once the pie is set, then serve.

NOTES: This makes 8 servings. You can use peanut butter and chopped roasted peanuts in place of the sunflower butter and sunflower seeds. You can serve with a dollop of whipped cream.

CRISPY BUÑUELOS

3 cups (400 g) all purpose flour
1 tsp (4 g) baking powder
1 tsp (5 g) salt
1/4 cup (60 g) lard or shortening
1 cup (236.59 ml) cinnamon tea
cooking oil for frying

TEA
1 1/2 cups (355 ml) water
1 cinnamon stick (5 g)
1 tsp (2.25 g) whole anise seed

SUGAR COATING
2 cups (400 g) sugar
1 Tbsp (4.5 g) ground cinnamon
1/4 tsp (1.25 g) fine salt (optional)

1. For the tea, add 1 1/2 cups water, cinnamon stick, and whole anise seeds to a small pot, and bring to a simmer. Cover with a lid, gently simmer for 10 minutes, turn off the heat and steep for 5 minutes. Strain and reserve 1 cup for the dough.

2. In a large bowl, combine flour, baking powder and salt. Next add lard and mix until flour becomes crumbly. Then add cinnamon tea and combine until a dough ball forms.

3. Place the dough ball on a clean lightly floured work surface and knead for 10 minutes. Then separate into 12 to 14 dough balls, place back into a bowl, cover with a damp cloth and rest for at least 15 minutes.

4. In a separate bowl, combine sugar, cinnamon and salt. Mix well and set aside.

5. Dust rolling pin and work surface with the extra flour. Roll out the dough into a thin circular shape at least 8 to 9 inches in diameter. Repeat the process until 3 or 4 are rolled out. Hang them on the side of the bowl to rest before frying.

6. Preheat a 12 inch pan filled with 1/2 inch of cooking oil to 350 °F / 176 °C.

7. Place the rolled out tortilla dough into the fry oil. Fry each side for at least 45 seconds or until fried dough is deep golden brown on each side. Cook time will vary.

8. Once the dough is fried, place on a baking sheet with a wire rack.

9. While the fried dough is still warm, dredge with the sugar cinnamon mixture on both sides. Then carefully place on a dish. Repeat until all are fried and dredged.

NOTES: This makes at least 12 buñuelos. A 1/4 cup of cooking oil can be substituted for the lard.

DARK CHOCOLATE CUPCAKES

1 1/2 cup (195 g) all purpose flour
1/2 tsp (2 g) baking powder
1 tsp (3 g) baking soda
1/2 tsp (2.5 g) salt
1/3 cup (33 g) unsweetened dark cocoa powder
1/2 cup (118 ml) whole milk
1/2 cup (120 g) sour cream
1 large egg
1 1/4 cup (250 g) sugar
1 tsp (4.9 ml) vanilla extract
1/3 cup (78 ml) cooking oil

1. In a bowl combine, flour, baking powder, baking soda, salt and cocoa powder. Mix well and set aside until needed.

2. In a separate large bow, combine milk, sour cream, egg, sugar, vanilla extract and cooking oil. Mix well.

3. Line a 12-cup muffin pan with baking cups and evenly distribute batter.

4. Bake in a preheated oven at 350 °F / 176 °C for 15 to 18 minutes or until an inserted toothpick comes out clean.

5. After the bake time, remove the cupcakes from the oven and transfer to a wire rack to cool.

6. Once the cupcakes have cooled to room temperature, use your favorite homemade or store bought frosting to top them. My **Easy Chocolate Ganache** recipe is perfect for these cupcakes.

NOTES: This makes at least 12 cupcakes.

EASY CHOCOLATE GANACHE FOR CUPCAKES

4 fl oz (118 ml) heavy cream
8 oz (227 g) semi sweet baking chocolate
1/4 tsp (1.25 ml) vanilla extract
1 Tbsp (14.2 g) salted butter (softened)

1. Add heavy cream to a microwave-safe bowl and heat in a microwave for 30 to 45 seconds or until hot.

2. Add chopped semi sweet baking chocolate to a heat proof bowl and pour the heated heavy cream over the chocolate. Do not stir and let it set for 10 minutes.

3. Now stir to combine, then add vanilla extract, softened butter and continue to mix well.

4. To ice the cupcakes, take one cupcake and dip the top into the bowl of ganache and place back on to the wire rack to allow the ganache to cool and set.

DAX'S CHOCOLATE CHIP COOKIES

1 1/2 cups (225 g) all purpose flour
1 tsp (5 g) baking soda
1 tsp (5 g) salt
8 Tbsp (113 g) unsalted butter (softened)
1 packed cup (200 g) dark brown sugar
1/4 cup (50 g) granulated sugar
1 room temperature large egg
1 1/2 tsp (7.5 ml) vanilla extract
6 oz (174 g) semi-sweet chocolate chips

1. In a bowl, add flour, baking soda and salt. Mix well and set aside until needed.

2. In a separate large bowl, combine butter, dark brown sugar, sugar, egg and vanilla extract. Cream together.

3. Combine the dry flour mixture into a creamy wet mixture, then fold in chocolate chips.

4. Cover and refrigerate the dough for at least 30 minutes to set.

5. On a baking sheet lined with parchment paper, using two spoons, add 1 1/2 Tbsp of cookie dough 2 inches apart.

6. Bake in a preheated oven at 350 °F / 176 °C for 12 to 14 minutes.

7. Once baked, remove from the oven, place cookies on a wire rack to cool and set for 15 minutes and then serve.

NOTES: This makes at least 18 to 20 cookies. You can substitute the dark brown sugar with light brown sugar.

EASY FRESH PEACH COBBLER

9 to 10 peaches (about 2 1/2 lbs)
1/3 cup (70 g) granulated sugar
1/4 tsp (1.25 g) salt
1 Tbsp (15 ml) fresh lemon juice
2 tsp (10 ml) vanilla extract
1/4 tsp ground cinnamon
a pinch of freshly grated nutmeg (optional)
1 Tbsp (7.5 g) cornstarch

DOUGH
2 cups (300 g) all purpose flour
1/2 cup (100 g) granulated sugar
2 tsp (8 g) baking powder
1 tsp (5 g) salt
8 Tbsp (113 g) cold unsalted butter
2 /3 cup (157 ml) mineral water

TOPPING
1/4 cup (50 g) granulated sugar
1/2 tsp (1.5 g) ground cinnamon

1. Cut 9 to 10 rinsed peaches in half and remove the pit from the center. Thinly slice peaches and place in a large bowl.

2. To the sliced peaches, add sugar, salt, lemon juice, vanilla extract, ground cinnamon, pinch of grated nutmeg and corn starch. Mix well.

3. In a separate bowl, combine flour, baking powder, salt and sugar. Mix well.

4. Now add cold unsalted butter and combine until the flour mixture is crumbly. Next add the mineral water and combine until a ball forms without overworking the dough.

CONTINUE TO PAGE 92

5. In a buttered 9 x 13 baking dish, add peaches, then top with hand torn flat pieces of dough.

6. In a small bowl, combine sugar and ground cinnamon. Sprinkle all over the top of the cobbler.

7. Bake in a preheated oven at 400 °F / 204 °C for 35 to 40 minutes.

8. Remove from the oven and let sit for 10 to 15 minutes. Then serve.

NOTES: This makes at least 8 servings. Serve warm with a scoop of your favorite vanilla ice cream.

SOFT PUMPKIN EMPANADAS

2 1/3 cup (300 g) all-purpose flour
1/3 cup (60 g) sugar
1 1/2 tsp (4 g) active dry yeast
1/4 tsp (1.25 g) salt
1 1/2 tsp (4.5 g) ground cinnamon
7 Tbsp (98 g) unsalted butter softened
2/3 cup (160 mL) warm milk
1 1/2 tsp (4.5 g) ground anise
extra flour

PUMPKIN FILLING

15 oz (425 g) pumpkin puree
3/4 cup (150 g) piloncillo or dark brown sugar
1/2 of a vanilla bean pod
1/4 (1.25 g) tsp salt
1/2 tsp (1.5 g) ground cinnamon
1/2 tsp 1.5 g) ground anise

MAKE THE FILLING

1. In a small pot on a low heat, combine pumpkin puree, piloncillo, vanilla bean caviar from the pod and scraped vanilla bean pod, salt, ground cinnamon and ground anise.

2. Once the filling mixture is bubbling and gently simmering, cover with a lid. Simmer on a low heat for 20 minutes. Be sure to stir throughout cook time.

3. Once the pumpkin filling has reduced and has become thick and paste-like, remove from heat and cool completely.

CONTINUE TO PAGE 94

MAKE THE EMPANADAS

1. In a large bowl, add flour, sugar, yeast, salt, ground cinnamon, ground anise, butter, warm milk and combine with clean hands. Mix in a bowl until a dough ball forms.

2. On a clean surface knead the dough for five minutes. Then divide into 14 dough balls.

3. Use extra flour for dusting the work surface and rolling pin. Now roll out the dough ball into a flat disc. Add 1 1/2 Tbsp pumpkin filling to the center, fold over and firmly press the edges to seal the empanada. Repeat the process.

4. Place the empanadas on a large baking sheet lined with parchment paper, cover with cling film and rest for 30 minutes.

5. Bake in a preheated oven at 350 °F / 176 °C for 20 to 25 minutes.

6. Once golden brown and baked, remove from the oven and allow to cool for 15 minutes then serve.

NOTES: This makes at least 12 empanadas. These can be stored in an airtight container for up to 3 days. These are best eaten within 48 hours.

WALNUT PECAN COOKIES

1 1/2 cups (225 g) all-purpose flour
1 tsp (5 g) baking soda
1 tsp (5 g) salt
8 Tbsp (113 g) unsalted butter softened
1 packed cup (200 g) dark brown sugar
1/4 cup (50 g) granulated sugar
1 room temperature large egg
1 1/2 tsp (7.5 ml) vanilla extract
1/2 cup (45 g) walnuts chopped
1/2 cup (45 g) pecans chopped

1. In a bowl, add flour, baking soda and salt. Mix well and set aside until needed.

2. In a separate large bowl, combine butter, dark brown sugar, sugar, egg and vanilla extract. Then cream together.

3. Combine the dry flour mixture into creamy wet mixture, then fold in walnuts and pecans.

4. Cover and refrigerate dough for at least 30 minutes to set.

5. On a baking sheet lined with parchment paper, using two spoons, add 1 1/2 Tbsp of cookie dough 2 inches apart.

6. Bake in a preheated oven at 350 °F / 176 °C for 12 to 14 minutes.

7. Once baked, remove from the oven, place cookies on a wire rack to cool and set for 15 minutes and then serve.

NOTES: This makes at least 24 cookies. You can use the chopped nuts of your choice. You can substitute the dark brown sugar with light brown sugar.

BEVERAGES

CREAMY CHAMPURRADO

4 cups (946 ml) water
1 cinnamon stick (5 g)
3 to 4 whole cloves
3 to 4 allspice berries
12 oz (354 ml) can evaporated milk
2 oz (56 g) piloncillo (or dark brown sugar)
3.1 oz (88 g) tablet of Mexican hot chocolate
1/3 cup (40 g) instant corn flour for masa
1/2 cup (118 ml) water
1/4 tsp (1.25 g) salt

1. In a pot, add 4 cups of water, cinnamon stick, whole cloves and allspice berries. Bring to a gentle boil, cover with a lid and gently simmer for 15 minutes.

2. Skim out the cinnamon stick, cloves and allspice berries.

3. Now add evaporated milk, piloncillo and the Mexican hot chocolate tablet. Bring to a gentle simmer and combine well.

4. In a cup, add instant corn flour for masa, salt and water. Mix until smooth and combine well to create a slurry.

5. Now pour the slurry into the simmering pot of liquid, mix and combine well.

6. Simmer for an additional 10 minutes, stirring occasionally. Then serve.

NOTES: You can substitute evaporated milk with whole milk. This serves at least 4 to 6.

CREAMY HORCHATA

1 cup (180 g) long grain rice
3 cups (709 ml) water
1 (5 g) stick of cinnamon
2 tsp (12 ml) vanilla extract
12 oz can (354 ml) evaporated milk
14 oz can (396 g) sweetened condensed milk
1 lb (454 g) ice

1. Wash and rinse the rice in cold water, then drain well.
2. In a bowl, add the rinsed rice, water and stick of cinnamon. Soak for at least 6 hours.
3. In a blender, add the entire bowl of soaked rice, cinnamon stick and soaking water.
4. Blend on high until the rice and the cinnamon stick are broken down.
5. Strain liquid from the blender through a fine wire mesh sieve into a large pitcher or jug.
6. Now add vanilla extract, evaporated milk and sweetened condensed milk. Stir well.
7. Next add ice, combine well and serve.

NOTES: You can substitute sweetened condensed milk for sugar to your taste combined with an extra can of evaporated milk. You can substitute the stick of cinnamon for 1/2 tsp of ground cinnamon. Be sure to add the ground cinnamon to the blender.

FRESH STRAWBERRY HORCHATA

1 cup (180 g) long grain rice
4 1/2 cups (1.06 L) water
1 (5 g) stick of cinnamon
1 lb (454 g) fresh strawberries
2 tsp (12 ml) vanilla extract
12 oz can (354 ml) evaporated milk
14 oz can (396 g) sweetened condensed milk
1 lb (454 g) ice

1. Wash and rinse the rice in cold water, then drain well.

2. In a bowl, add the rinsed rice, 2 1/2 cups water and the cinnamon stick. Soak for at least 6 hours.

3. In a blender, add the entire bowl of soaked rice, cinnamon stick and soaking water.

4. Blend on high until the rice and the cinnamon stick are broken down.

5. Strain liquid from the blender through a fine wire mesh sieve into a large pitcher or jug.

6. Remove the tops from the strawberries, chop, add to the blender with 2 cups of water and puree.

7. Pour strawberry puree through fine wire mesh strainer and add to pitcher.

8. Now add evaporated milk, sweetened condensed milk and vanilla extract. Stir well.

9. Next add ice, combine well and serve.

NOTES: You can substitute sweetened condensed milk for sugar to your taste combined with an extra can of evaporated milk. You can substitute the stick of cinnamon for 1/4 tsp to 1/2 tsp of ground cinnamon. Be sure to add the ground cinnamon to the blender.

FRESH BANANA MILK

8 cups (1.9 L) cold water
2 ripe bananas (310 g)
2 tsp (12 ml) vanilla extract
1/4 tsp (.75 g) ground cinnamon
14 oz (396 g) sweetened condensed milk
12 fl oz (354 ml) evaporated milk
4 cups (946 ml) cold water
1 lb (454 g) ice

1. In a blender, add 4 cups of water, chopped bananas, vanilla extract and ground cinnamon. Blend until smooth and creamy.
2. Pour the banana mixture into a pitcher.
3. Add 4 cups of water, sweetened condensed milk and evaporated milk. Mix well.
4. Next add ice, combine well and serve.

NOTES: You can substitute sweetened condensed milk for sugar to your taste combined with an extra can of evaporated milk. You can substitute evaporated milk with whole milk.

ACKNOWLEDGMENTS

I want to give special thanks to those that have helped me, inspired me or given me a bit of kindness to keep me going. There are so many people who have supported me along the way. I want to acknowledge that this book is through the efforts and encouragement of many.

First, I would like to thank my husband Chaeyik. You were the first person to encourage me to share my recipes. You came up with the name Gochujang Mamá which embraced our multicultural family and in turn started our social media endeavors. You also were right there to taste test my many successes and many failures in the kitchen. You are the real M.V.P. and G.O.A.T. Thank you for your support, guidance and love. We have certainly come a long way, and I look forward to more adventures together in and out of the kitchen. Te amo Yeobo.

To my sons, Dax and Bo, thank you for inspiring me daily. You both teach me that learning is a process best enjoyed and embraced. There is never a dull moment. You keep me on my toes. You also remind me that I have the best full-time, all-the-time job in the world. I am your Mamá. I love you both, and I hope you will treasure the meals that I cook for you. I will always try to measure and notate what I make. Maybe one day you can recreate a delicious, home-cooked meal and think back on a treasured family memory. I love you both beyond measure, infinitely and even more than that.

To all of my family and friends, if you have ever cooked or treated me to a meal, thank you. You have truly blessed me with nourishment, good company and, most of all, kindness. You also may have inspired a recipe in this book.

To my followers and supporters thank you all. You may know me as Gochujang Mamá or as Simply Mamá Cooks. Just know that I am grateful for your constant support and kind words. As always, I hope you like these recipes. I hope you give them a try, and thanks for watching!

To my Dad, you are truly missed. Thank you for inspiring my recipe for fideo con pollo and teaching me an easy method for a quick Mexican style rice. By the way, I finally made a damn cookbook. Love ya, Pops.

CREDITS

Page 7: photo by Chaeyik Jung; Page 9: rolling pin illustration by Liudmila Kopecka/Shutterstock.com, chilli pepper illustrations by Ann Merrow/Shutterstock.com, corn illustration by Elena Pimonova/Shutterstock.com; Page 13: jalapeño illustration by Daria Ustiugova/Shutterstock.com, avocado, tomato and onion illustrations by Elena Pimonova/Shutterstock.com; Page 19: chicken leg with parsley illustration by nld/Shutterstock.com, onion illustration by Elena Pimonova/Shutterstock.com; Page 57: pan with fresh vegetables illustration by Daria Ustiugova/Shutterstock.com; Page 75: bell pepper illustration by Elena Pimonova/Shutterstock.com, onion illustration by Elena Pimonova/Shutterstock.com, cilantro illustration by Daria Ustiugova/Shutterstock.com; Page 83: peach illustrations by Elena Pimonova/Shutterstock.com, rolling pin illustration by Liudmila Kopecka/Shutterstock.com, cinnamon illustration by Anna Suprunenko/Shutterstock.com; Page 97: banana and strawberry illustrations by Sketch Master/Shutterstock.com, jug illustration by Iya Balushkina/Shutterstock.com, cinnamon illustration by Anna Suprunenko/Shutterstock.com; Page 108: photo by Chaeyik Jung.

INDEX

JALAPEÑO
Roasted Guacamole Dip **14**
Easy Roasted Green Salsa **16**
Easy Everyday Salsa **17**
Mama's Fake-Out Guacamole Salsa **18**
Mama's Jalapeño Cheese Cornbread **51**
Mexican Style Pork with Squash **72**
Simple Charro Beans **77**

LIME
Roasted Guacamole Dip **14**
Stovetop Carne Asada **21**
Zesty Cilantro Lime Rice **79**

MACARONI
Creamy Stovetop Mac and Cheese **80**
Cream Spicy Mac and Cheese **81**

MEXICAN SQUASH
Mama's Fake-Out Guacamole Salsa **18**
Mexican Style Chicken Soup **68**
Mexican Style Beef Soup **70**
Mexican Style Pork with Squash **72**

MOLÉ
CJ's Favorite Molé Sauce **36**

MUSHROOM
Creamy Garlic Mushroom Chicken **38**

PASILLA CHILE
Tender Meat Filled Tamales **32**
CJ's Favorite Molé Sauce **36**
Easy Slow Cooker Beef Birria **58**

PASTA
Pop's Fideo con Pollo **45**
Creamy Stovetop Mac and Cheese **80**
Creamy Spicy Mac and Cheese **81**

PEACH
Easy Fresh Peach Cobbler **91**

PECAN
Walnut Pecan Cookies **95**

POBLANO PEPPER
Crispy Chile Rellenos **40**
Easy Chicken Pozole Verde **66**

PORK
Tender Meat Filled Tamales **32**
Easy Mexican Style Chorizo **44**
Simple Slow Cooker Pork Shoulder **47**
Easy Red Pork Pozole **62**
Mexican Style Pork with Squash **72**

POTATO
Crispy Chile Rellenos **40**
Easy Picadillo for Tacos **42**
Pop's Fideo con Pollo **45**
Mexican Style Chicken Soup **68**
Mexican Style Beef Soup **70**

PUMPKIN
Soft Pumpkin Empanadas **93**

PUMPKIN SEEDS
Easy Chicken Pozole Verde **66**

RICE
Mama's Arroz Con Pollo **26**
Easy Mexican Style Rice **76**
Easy Homemade Yellow Rice **78**
Zesty Cilantro Lime Rice **79**
Abuelita's Arroz con Leche **84**
Creamy Horchata **99**
Fresh Strawberry Horchata **100**

ROMA TOMATO
Roasted Guacamole Dip **14**
Easy Roasted Green Salsa **16**
Stovetop Carne Guisada **20**
CJ's Favorite Molé Sauce **36**
Simple Charro Beans **77**

SALSA
see Salsas and Dips **13**

SAUCE
Tex-Mex Ground Beef Enchiladas,
  red sauce **24**
Simple Stovetop Red Enchiladas,
  red sauce **30**
CJ's Favorite Molé Sauce **36**
Simple Oven Baked BBQ Chicken,
  bbq sauce **52**

SLOW COOKER
Simple Slow Cooker Pork Shoulder **47**
Simple Slow Cooker Beef Chuck Roast **48**
Simple Slow Cooker Beef Barbacoa **49**
Easy Slow Cooker Beef Birria **58**

SOUP
see Soups and Stews **57**

STRAWBERRY
Fresh Strawberry Horchata **100**

SUNFLOWER BUTTER
CJ's Favorite Molé Sauce **36**
Bo's Sunflower Butter Chocolate Pie **85**

TAMALES
Tender Meat Filled Tamales **32**

TOMATILLO
Mama's Favorite Salsa **15**
Easy Roasted Green Salsa **16**
Mama's Fake-Out Guacamole Salsa **18**
CJ's Favorite Molé Sauce **36**
Easy Chicken Pozole Verde **66**

WALNUT
Walnut Pecan Cookies **95**

ZUCCHINI
Easy Picadillo for Tacos **42**
Pop's Fideo con Pollo **45**

ABOUT THE AUTHOR

Angelica Faz Jung was born and resides in Texas. A wife and mother to two boys, she is a home cook with a passion for feeding family and friends. Her love of cooking developed at an early age. Pulling from her Mexican American heritage, Angelica finds inspiration for many of her recipes from dishes prepared around her grandmothers' tables growing up as well as family favorites. When she's not cooking, she enjoys spending time with friends or watching classic movies with her husband and sons.

Lightning Source UK Ltd.
Milton Keynes UK
UKHW021111090820
367868UK00008B/177